ENDORSEMENTS

Finding Normal in Bipolar is more than a story—it's a lifeline. Teresa Brunsting opens her heart with such raw honesty and grace that you can't help but feel seen, understood, and deeply moved. She gives voice to the silent battles so many face, weaving her journey through pain, faith, and healing with courage and compassion.

What I love most about Teresa's writing is her steadfast hope in God's redemptive power. Even in her darkest valleys, she invites the reader to witness how the Lord met her there—restoring peace where despair once lived, and giving her purpose where shame once spoke loudest.

This book isn't just for those navigating bipolar disorder—it's for families, friends, and anyone longing to understand how faith and mental health can coexist in God's story of healing. Teresa's transparency helps lift the stigma, while her faith points us all back to the One who makes wholeness possible.

Finding Normal in Bipolar is a brave, necessary, and beautifully redemptive read.

— Niccie Kliegl, CEO, Fulfill Your Legacy; Spiritual Growth & Leadership Coach, Speaker; Author of the Legacy Series

Finding Normal in Bipolar is a courageous and beautifully honest story of overcoming mental health challenges during the fiercest storms of life. Teresa Brunsting invites readers into her journey—not only as a woman learning to manage bipolar disorder, but as a wife and mother determined not to be defined by it.

With raw, vulnerable, and spiritual depth, Teresa offers a profound glimpse into the realities of living with bipolar disorder while navigating deeply painful life events. What makes this story especially powerful is its rare, holistic perspective—the reader is welcomed into the hearts of her husband and children as well. Their shared experiences reveal how mental health affects an entire family and how faith, empathy, and love can lead to true healing and restoration.

I love this book. The truths Teresa shares are profound and timeless. Her lessons on forgiveness, identity, perseverance, grace, and unconditional love speak to families facing life's storms.

If you are hoping for a book that will touch your heart and deepen your empathy for those you love, look no further. This book will encourage and strengthen you on your own journey beside the people you hold dear.

—Donna Bess, Award-Winning Author of *Sidetracked to Surrender: A True Story of Overcoming Trials and Finding Redemption in God's Love*

Finding Normal in Bipolar is a gripping autobiography of bipolar reality. If your interest expands beyond the psychology of the struggle to the lived experience, this is a must read. Brunsting's transparency and learned self-awareness provides an engaging narrative for anyone grappling with the realities of bipolar disorder. Refreshing, even in the retelling of painful family situations, this book offers hope for normalizing life with faith and determination. The picture painted is not always pretty, but it is honest, and that is what makes her work relatable and inspiring. Anyone who has struggled with a significant mental health issue will struggle to put the book down. Turn the page and enter the world of hurt, and of realistic hope.

—**Fred DeJong, Lead Pastor, First Reformed Church, Orange City, Iowa**

FINDING NORMAL ⓘ BIPOLAR

Leveling My Mind and Becoming My
True Self with God's Love and Peace

by

TERESA BRUNSTING

Light Warrior
PUBLISHING ™

FINDING NORMAL IN BIPOLAR: Leveling My Mind and Becoming My
True Self with God's Love and Peace ©2025 by Teresa Brunsting

Published by: Light Warrior Publishing, Franklin, TN
Editor: Loral Pepoon, loralpepoon.com
Cover Design: Tammy Largin

ISBNs: paperback 978-1-969202-14-8
e-book 978-1-969202-15-5
hardback 978-1-969202-16-2

Disclaimer: The conversations in this book all come from the author's recollections. They are not written to represent word-for-word transcripts. Rather, the author has re-told them in a way that evokes the feeling and meaning of what was said. In all instances, the essence of the dialogue is a close and accurate account of what took place. The author has changed the names of several individuals and places and may have changed some identifying characteristics and details for the protection of many in this book.

A Prayer for Those Trying to Find "Normal" with Bipolar

Dear Heavenly Father,

I pray this book will help my readers and their families navigate bipolar or other mental illnesses so that they can find a new normal. I ask for Your special touch on people everywhere who are suffering from this burden or from accompanying discouragement. Help them not to despair but to trust in Your goodness. Encourage my readers and reveal to them the pieces of my story that might connect to their own journeys.

Thank You, God, for always being there for me. There were times I thought I was alone, but You were there to guide me all along. Healing took time for me, but it was worth the wait for Your timing, God. Thank You for giving me the passion and desire to share my story with others.

I also pray that my readers experience joy in Your strength. I pray that they, like me, become free as they embrace the healing and forgiveness Your Son offers them. I thank You for Your steadfast love, and I ask that this book will help readers want to experience Your perfect love that brings peace.

I pray my story will help them see how You may be guiding them to put together a new narrative from their struggle with mental illness. I ask that You not only equip them as they embark on a journey of finding normal in bipolar but that in the process, You help them emulate Your love in their spheres of influence.

In Jesus' Name I pray,

Amen

I dedicate this book first and foremost to the Father, Son, and Holy Spirit, who make all things possible.

To my family: To my husband, Doug, we have weathered some storms and are now happily growing older together. You have become one of my biggest supporters in my writing journey, and I'm so grateful for your unwavering love and patience, especially for holding down the fort while I disappeared into my writing world.

To my children, Cooper and Olivia: you inspire me every day with your resilience and your reminders of what matters most. Cooper, you are a kind and generous man who makes me proud every day. Olivia, who came to us at five months old from South Korea, you have blessed our lives from the very beginning. You are an amazing writer and editor. You are the reason I first began connecting with authors and the publishing world.

FOREWORD

When I first read Teresa Brunsting's story, **Finding "Normal" in Bipolar.** I felt like I was being invited into the most honest and tender parts of her life. She doesn't hold back. She takes us with her as a little girl, watching her mom's emotions change in a moment—from explosive anger to calm as if nothing happened. Later, she shares her own journey of not understanding why her emotions felt out of control, and then the heartbreaking discovery that she was living with bipolar disorder.

Teresa writes with such openness that you don't just learn about bipolar—you *feel* it. You feel the chaos, the longing to just be "normal," and the fight to keep going when life feels unbearable. She even brings us to the night she attempted to end her life, and then the moment of truth that led to her diagnosis. Reading her words, I could see not only her bravery, but also the deep love she has for those who might be walking this road too.

Her story also gave me something I wasn't expecting— compassion. I realized, as I read, that most likely my own mother was living with undiagnosed bipolar disorder. As a child, all I knew was the unpredictability. Now, through Teresa's story, I can see my mom differently. I can imagine the battle she was fighting inside, and I can hold her memory with more understanding and grace.

That's why I believe this book is such a gift. If you have someone in your life who may be struggling with bipolar, or if you've ever wondered how to understand what's happening in their world, this book will help you. Teresa doesn't give you a medical textbook—she gives you her heart. And that makes all the difference.

I pray this book finds its way into many hands. I hope it brings light, hope, and understanding to families and friends who don't yet have the words for what they're experiencing. And I hope, one day, we can look back and see that stories like Teresa's helped move us toward a world where mental illness is no longer hidden in silence, but met with compassion, courage, and healing.

—Missy Maxwell Worton, Award-Winning Author of *Don't Mess With This Mama*, President of Warrior Writer Training & Light Warrior Publishing

CONTENTS

Chapter One

TRYING TO END IT ALL

I longed for peace. I longed for silence.

I found myself lying on the shag carpet under my kitchen table with empty bottles next to me. It felt good to feel the table leg against my back as I curled up in a fetal position. I almost felt like my body was starting to float, and my mind felt numb. It was in a strange way, refreshing. I had become exhausted trying to be the person everyone wanted and expected me to be for what seemed like forever.

Earlier that day, I was keenly aware of the date—December 15, 1986—four days before my twenty-fifth birthday. I felt the sting of realizing my birthday would once again not be celebrated as its own occasion. The feeling of being overlooked since everyone was always busy with Christmas plans seemed even more intense than it had in previous years.

A few minutes before I was on the floor, I had made up my mind; I just didn't want to deal with the overwhelming disappointment I felt—not just about my birthday, but about my entire life. I had a decent job, a boyfriend, and good friends, so the severity of my feelings didn't make sense to me—or to anyone else.

1

I had wrestled with the thought of using some method to stop the pain during the previous few years many times. But on that particular day, I decided to take all the pills my doctor had prescribed for anxiety, along with some over-the-counter drugs, to numb my overwhelming emotions. My mind and my body wanted to give up on life.

I remember feeling cold lying there under the table, noticing that my breathing was staggered and slow. My apartment in Lamoni, Iowa, was eerily quiet, and finally, my body felt the momentary peace I longed for after I could no longer move. My thoughts began to wander like a film rattling through a projector, as if a movie was playing highlights of my life. I started to drift deeper into my own thoughts.

Suddenly, I heard a loud noise. My front door had been busted open, and two men were pulling me out from under the table.

"Open your eyes," one of the men said loudly with urgency as he picked me up and positioned me on a stretcher. Can you hear me?"

The other man echoed his counterpart, "Can you hear me?"

Even though I could hear them, I wasn't able to open my eyes or respond. Sometime between leaving my apartment and being maneuvered into the ambulance, I could feel the paramedics begin to work on my body, trying to get me to respond ...

I lost consciousness.

Chapter Two

AWAKENING TO DIFFICULT CONVERSATIONS

I awoke to bright lights. I could hear the sound of medical equipment beeping and people talking. I wondered if I had died. I couldn't understand what was being said, but I heard people's voices again. *Are they talking to me?* Confused, I drifted off.

As I woke up again, I realized that I was in the hospital with my family surrounding me. I learned that when I didn't show up for work that morning at Graceland College's Publication Center, my co-workers became concerned. My boss and the EMT were the ones who broke into my apartment to rescue me. By the grace of God, who must have prompted their actions, they found me before it was too late.

I remember thinking as I was lying in my hospital bed, *Why am I still here? I must have a purpose.* I didn't, however, have a sense of purpose with all the chaos in my mind. In fact, I had never understood the reason I was created.

What I did know was that the emergence of the heightened emotions that started in high school was continuing to disrupt my life well into young adulthood. And, on that day, at almost twenty-five, I had attempted suicide.

I can remember thinking: *I really need help. What have I done?*

I also knew that my family was glad to see me, and I was glad to see them.

Clearly shaken, Mom said, "We are so glad you're okay, Teresa. You worried us."

I looked at my dad, who had the same concerned look on his face as my mom. I could see tears in his eyes.

I do have to admit, though, I felt a little anger and disbelief that no one had known how miserable I was before it had gotten that bad. I wish those closest to me had tried to stop me from getting to the point of being suicidal.

But then I thought, *How could they have known since I hadn't told them what I had been going through? What could I have told them anyway, since I didn't really understand why I was having these intense emotions?*

Dr. Singh, a psychiatrist, added to my confusion with a barrage of questions and testing. Later that week, he told me that the synapses in my brain were not connecting properly, and he diagnosed me with bipolar 1 disorder.[1] What that basically meant is that I had a chemical imbalance that accentuated my emotions —both good and bad. I felt like a ping-pong ball bouncing back and forth. The intensity of emotions and thoughts of suicide were overwhelming because of the misfiring of my brain.

For the few days that I was in the hospital after my suicide attempt, I had an IV in my arm and wore a heart monitor to make sure my breathing and heart rate were returning to normal. I felt relieved when the nurses started doing progressive relaxation with me twice a day. Not only did I learn to deal with my immediate emotions, but I began to have hope because I realized I could use this relaxation technique on my own to help me move forward.

I also went to group counseling, which made me feel that I wasn't alone in how I felt. In addition to group education and discussion, we engaged our creativity by making crafts. The relaxation techniques and creative activities calmed my mind and settled impulsive and heightened emotions. Dr. Singh had explained that the "high" or impulsive side of the bipolar emotional cycle was called mania, which for me could include irritability and high energy.

As I started to learn a bit more about bipolar in the hospital, I began to wonder, *Are my issues genetic, or are some of them because of traumas that I had experienced growing up?* I didn't yet have the answers I wanted, but I realized that to survive, I not only had much to learn about the origins of my illness, but I also needed to learn how to cope with it. My severe responses made a little more sense with a label.

But the question on repeat most often remained: *Why am I still here?* A secondary one was, *Why does God think I can handle this life?*

I remembered Grandma saying, "God won't give you any more than you can handle."

His confidence, however, when I felt none, only increased my sense of unworthiness and barraged my mind with more questions.

Why couldn't I just be normal?

*Why didn't **He** enable me to handle everything?*

Four days after my suicide attempt on my actual twenty-fifth birthday, I was still in the hospital. My boyfriend, Adam, and another couple asked if I would want to go out to a restaurant with them to mark the occasion. I was thankful to be granted a two-hour release. I wasn't in charge of my own time during that mandatory week stay, but it was good to see friends in a "normal" environment.

They wanted to know all about what had happened. I could sense they felt bad as the questions began.

Adam started the conversation with the expected question, "Are you going to be okay?"

"What is it like to have bipolar?" Russell asked.

And Sarah, a bit more empathetic and perhaps feeling some regret, added, "We didn't know you were so sad."

I answered by trying to explain a little of what I had learned in the hospital: "If you have bipolar, you feel like you are going down a road you didn't choose. You don't know when it will end —or if it ever will, and you want a way out. Any way out sometimes will do. You just want peace."

I went on to share more. "I also learned that bipolar often emerges in late teens and early twenties. Your emotions change, and it's confusing because, in your heart, you are the same person people used to love and appreciate."

It was hard for my friends to understand, and I felt sympathy for them because I was still struggling to understand how bipolar worked too.

My friends weren't the only people who I would need to deal with as I learned more about this diagnosis; I would also need to involve my parents. In the family counseling that Dr. Singh had us start, we discovered that my mom had emotional struggles like I did. She too was diagnosed with bipolar disorder. Several sessions later, we also realized that Mom's father had the same characteristics of highs and lows. I then knew, without a doubt, that what I was experiencing was genetically passed down to me.

After a mandatory week-long stay at the hospital, I was released and went with my parents to my apartment in Lamoni to get some clothes. Going in the apartment initially gave me an intense feeling of remorse and sadness.

Mom and Dad were very concerned about me, and Mom suggested, "Why don't you come stay with us for a few days and we can make you some good food and you can rest over Christmas?"

I replied, "I know that I need to follow the directions of the doctors and work toward a better future with God's help. I need to wrap my mind around taking this medication and make plans for follow-up counseling to get healthy." *Could I do it?* I thought. *This will take a lot of discipline.*

I continued processing what came next with my parents, "I know I'll have to build a routine to become healthier emotionally, and once I get there, that will take work on my part to maintain. I'm willing to do the work, but I'm still shaky and unsure of how life will move forward."

"That's why you should come home for Christmas", Mom said.

"Okay, I'll come," I said. I decided to stay for four or five days —at least till I could get some rest, see more of my family members, start to establish new disciplines, and feel more steady.

As I spent time with family, I realized that my suicide attempt definitely shook everyone's confidence in me taking care of myself which was easy for me to understand.

I relished the opportunity to rest, enjoy home cooking, and to be with family to make new Christmas memories. The heavy weight of what I had done began to be replaced with "normal" activities, and I began to have hope that I could move forward with internal normalcy.

Every night when I was staying with my parents, I would talk to Adam. He and I had been seeing each other for over a year. I was a little unsure how what I had done would affect our relationship, but he invited me to come visit his family over our break. I think he also wanted to take me home so he could keep an eye on me.

I agreed. Right after Christmas at home, I rode ten hours with Adam to Pontiac, Michigan, to visit his parents. I had thought I was strong enough to go, even though I still felt weak. While I was there, however, I ended up in the hospital again—this time in the ER with pneumonia. I received strong antibiotics and fluids and was released several hours later. I was glad to be able to recover at Adam's parents for a week.

After the first of the year, I returned to work. Because I was still emotionally a little shaky, it was hard getting back into the swing of life, but I really liked my job.

I had worked my way up to be assistant manager, and I enjoyed not just the work that I did at the publications center, but I also liked the co-workers and students that I interacted with.

Every day, Adam would come to my workplace to visit me on my break. He also knew many of the students who were completing their work study at the center, so I knew he wasn't just there to see me.

Adam must feel like a caregiver now, I often thought.

A few weeks after I had been back at work, Adam and I talked about the need to reconsider our relationship. We were the same age, although he was still a student. He would be graduating in a few months, and he needed to figure out his life. I really needed to work on myself alone. We walked around campus and talked about how my suicide attempt and repeat hospitalizations were a lot to handle. He knew he would be moving into the workplace after graduation, and he realized his life would become even busier. Though there were many tears, we knew it was best for us to part ways.

Dealing with this diagnosis felt like a life sentence that I did not want. Despite how I felt, I had to learn how to deal with the mental illness on top of normal life challenges. I worked hard to do what the doctors were telling me to do to move forward. They told me my ability to cope with the illness was up to me.

With the medication, taking care of myself, and making sure the people I was associating with were good for me, I began to get better little by little. The diagnosis gave me some clarity about the confusion in my mind, but I also needed to go back and look at everything that had gotten me to the point of giving up and ending it all. I recognized that I had much to unpack and sort through. As I started to examine my memories piece by piece, my emotions started to stabilize. I would have to learn how to deal with the traumas and the illness that seemed to augment them.

Chapter Three

REVISITING CHILDHOOD

As I mentioned, one of the first steps to begin the healing process after my diagnosis and suicide attempt was going to family counseling sessions with my parents. Over the course of six months, we had about eight one-hour sessions with a family therapist. During that season of life, we revisited some aspects of my childhood issues that would need to be understood and dealt with to help me find a path to normalcy.

In addition to finding more out about how my illness affected me in these sessions, I also learned how my mom's diagnosis of bipolar 2 disorder[2] contributed to some of the chaos in our home as I was growing up. Her emotions were depressed without mania, meaning she didn't have the racing thoughts and impulsivity that I had. Mom was often moody and irritable, which can be present in people with both bipolar 1 and bipolar 2.

I also learned that in both bipolar 1 and sometimes in bipolar 2, it could produce an unnatural or heightened reaction. The situation many times resulted in anger and saying harsh things only to have regret afterwards. Our diagnoses were different; our behaviors and responses for both my mom and me were similar, even if the causes were slightly different. *There was so much to learn about all this!*

I also was taught that triggers were different than a bipolar episode. A trigger could be something that happens that brings up a past hurt that causes emotions to flair in a way that may not correlate to the current circumstances. Triggers happen to everyone at times. A bipolar episode happens when extreme emotions surface because of a chemical imbalance and those emotions affect daily functioning. When someone with bipolar disorder also experiences a trigger, emotions can skyrocket out of control.

It was good, in a way, to learn from our therapist that the emotions that my mom and I both felt over the years were not our fault. Or at least not all of them. Some of them came from the chemical imbalance we faced with bipolar.

The therapist had us look back at any traumas or signs in childhood to help us differentiate between what reactions were from the disorder and what current reactions were from a trigger from the past.

As part of the looking back process, Mom shared more about her experience as a new mom. One of the earliest stories that sticks out is her sharing how she dealt with me as a small baby. I was crying and wouldn't stop. She said that I was so upset that I held my breath and started to turn blue. She threw cold water in my face to get me to gasp and breathe. I asked her why she didn't pick me up and comfort me, and she said that she was afraid she would hurt me. Because of her own emotions, she must have had a "freeze" reaction, meaning she was too overwhelmed to process what to do so she did nothing.

We also talked about the fact that I didn't have any siblings for nearly five years. Because my brother was due to be born in October, and Mom would need to focus on taking care of a newborn, Mom and Dad sent me to kindergarten when I was only four. Although she mentioned in a session that she thought I was smart enough, I know I wasn't emotionally ready. That fact was obvious to me because in my kindergarten group picture, I am sucking my thumb.

I also mentioned in counseling that I had always wondered if Mom's sadness was my fault. Hearing what was happening to her was insightful, and it helped me realize how she had acted was not my fault. I realized that she couldn't handle the situation and did the best that she could.

I also realized in therapy that my experience as a baby could have been the beginning of why I would sometimes hyperventilate and not be able to catch my breath when I was upset or crying. In doing research for this book, I learned that, according to Bowlby and Ainsworth's attachment theory, the way a caregiver responds to a baby's distress (like crying) helps shape that child's ability to regulate emotions either good or bad. If a baby repeatedly cries and is not soothed or held, they can develop an insecure attachment style. This lack of attachment may later manifest as difficulty regulating emotions, heightened stress response, and fear of abandonment. Adult reactions like panic attacks or hyperventilation may also be a result of an insecure attachment style.[3]

The family counseling for six months was an intensive learning time, but it was only the starting line on my road to healing. I continued to rely on counseling through my life. I would need to process much more about my background and the symptoms resulting from my attachment style and bipolar over time in years of therapy. I'll reveal more of that journey throughout this book.

First though, I'd like to share more about my upbringing and years leading up to my diagnosis. My hope is that if any of you see these signs in your children or other kids you know, perhaps you may be able to encourage them or their parents to seek help earlier in the journey.

As I started to share earlier, I went to school at four, and I believe being there too early contributed to my lack of success. My report cards said something like, "She could do the work if she applied herself, but she daydreams, and we always catch her looking out the window instead of doing her work. She seems very distracted."

I had extreme difficulties concentrating and applying what was taught. I was also often distracted by children at recess playing outside the window on the playground. I wanted to play more than learn during my early elementary school years.

I also remember being scared at school because the teachers were hard on me, pointing out that I wasn't reading and doing the work that most of my peers were. Because I went to school at an earlier age than most, I was perpetually trying to catch up with other kids, most of whom were a year older than me. I had a hard time reading and committing things to memory in early elementary school through third grade. I also needed to hear things more often than others for them to sink in. I was able to move from one grade to the next—just not with flying colors.

I also struggled especially in math and sometimes science. My mind was more on the creative or right side. I was shy, timid, and unsure of myself. My feeling of being perpetually behind likely contributed to me having nightmares about getting caught with my homework not being done and getting called on when I didn't know the answer.

In addition to feeling behind and wanting to play more, I was also sensitive about what was said—even when the words weren't about me. I remember the teacher praising others, saying, "Great work all of you who reached your goals in reading." The words about others stuck with me, even though they weren't said directly to me or intended to do me harm. They reinforced the negative words I had heard about my own abilities.

Academics weren't the only facet of school that was hard for me. I often watched the other kids play well together, and I felt like an outsider. I wanted to feel part of the group. *Why didn't I fit in?*

I also didn't feel comfortable in my own skin at home. I felt unworthy at home because I drew the false conclusion that I was a burden to my parents. My dad would talk about his day at the dinner table and speak with anger because he was frustrated about his day. I would internalize his frustration to the point that my stomach hurt, which made me lose my appetite. As a child, I didn't realize that he was unwinding from his work day and that his words had nothing to do with me but instead, they were about his work week and stress. Saturday was much better for Dad when he could focus on his hobbies and things around the house.

Because Mom had many headaches and needed to rest much of the time, I spent a good portion of my time, in the summer and on weekends, with Dad. We did fun activities together. He was very outdoorsy, so I spent time with him outside and in the garden. Sometimes we even went fishing. I felt important when I helped him with these activities because they provided food for our dinner table. Garden vegetables and fish were a treat for our family. My mom would can and freeze what we couldn't use right away. I enjoyed being Dad's little sidekick and helper. I remember liking to pull weeds and eat raw vegetables freshly picked.

When I wasn't with my dad doing one of these useful activities, I felt a little bit like a weed myself, just popping up anywhere like the ones in my Dad's garden. Many times, I wished I was more tended to. Decades later, I realized Dad was busy working and mom was dealing with her own illness. But also part of the reason I was by myself was that in small towns like mine, in the '60s and '70s, parents allowed their children to go out to play and have an adventure for an entire day in the summer or on the weekends when it wasn't too cold. We knew we had to be home for the evening meal before dark and not to be late.

After we ate and cleaned up from dinner, it was eventually just me and Dad. Mom went to bed early partly because of her headaches but also from being tired from taking care of my brother and working around the house. Dad and I would watch whatever sports or favorite movies or shows he liked at the time. I didn't really have a bedtime. I would just stay up with Dad and watch television. In fact, even when I was in elementary school, I was often still awake when the national anthem played at midnight, when one of the three network stations that we had on our TV went off the air. The late nights didn't help me in school; I usually didn't get enough sleep. Dad would fall asleep on the couch or in the chair, but like I said, I was his sidekick and longed for his company and approval, so I stayed there with him.

Because of the excessive TV watching, I thought I wanted to be an actress. I put on shows for my family. When I was pretending or acting, I was bold and outgoing. I started out being this confident character around my family members because they were safe.

I slowly decided that I should carry that confidence over to other parts of my life. I created a "character" Toni. I had watched an actor named Tony Curtis in several movies that my dad liked. He was charming and everyone liked him. I wanted to be the female version of these funny and confident characters Tony the actor portrayed. I wanted to be someone everyone liked too. So, although I never told anyone, I called myself Toni with an "I" since that was a girl's name. *I was now an actor too*, I thought.

Though it was scary, I first used Toni outside my family with friends at school on the playground. I never told anyone that I was doing this. Acting confident and being Toni helped me be more at ease in most situations—but I was a fake. I remember using Toni when I was around the neighborhood kids too. If I acted like Toni, they thought I was confident and seemed to pay more attention to me. When we played Red Rover, if I acted funny and outgoing, I was picked earlier for the teams. I liked the way being chosen sooner made me feel.

I enjoyed the positive reinforcement, so I kept using Toni to mask my insecurity. Masks serve many purposes, and mine helped me feel more seen, loved, worthy, and purposeful. As I began to experience those feelings of purpose, it helped me sense what I longed for—being normal.

I was becoming more popular with my "character" even though many times I would still go home and cry alone in my room.

Were my friends really my friends, or did they just like me because I was pretending, and they liked Toni?

Ironically, being Toni worked. She could say anything and be funny and entertaining. What I really wanted, though, was just to be loved and appreciated for being myself—Teresa.

There was a place I was loved unconditionally, however, where I didn't have to pretend to be someone else to be accepted —at my grandma's farm. As a kid, I was drawn to a certain tranquility being around the dogs and farm animals. I loved to watch my grandpa milk the cows and squirt milk at the cats. I enjoyed the wide-open spaces to explore.

Grandma was often my babysitter, and our family would go there on Sundays for dinner. I loved Grandma's mashed potatoes, and I was especially happy that she always let me mash them for her. We picked the potatoes from her garden every year and stored them in the root cellar so she always had them handy.

Not only did I love Grandma's unconditional love at her house, but I also loved somewhere I went with her: Sunday school and church. I can still remember being seven and enjoying the hymns—especially "Amazing Grace"—when they sang it in that old country church. I thought the Bible stories I was learning were fascinating. Looking back, I know the Holy Spirit started working on me in those classes. I fell in love with God and Jesus, and I had the faith of a child.

After church, Grandma and I would talk about what I had learned at Sunday school. During one of those conversations, Grandma said, "God won't give you any more than you can handle." That statement stuck with me.

When I started having emotional issues in my late teens several years prior to my suicide attempt, I would often wonder why God thought I was strong enough to handle life. Being with Grandma, however, always made me feel strong because I felt loved and worthy. I felt that way when I was with her because she showed me kindness and treated me like I was important.

To this day, I can also remember her saying to me as a young child, "Where's Teresa Lynn, Where's my little helper?"

Those words got my heart pounding—in a good way.

I would answer, "What do you need me to do?" Depending on the time of year, I also responded with, "Could I help you pick potatoes and carrots from the garden or help you cook?"

My grandma, my father's mother, was the one who instilled gardening into my dad, and I wanted to continue that work and help both of them—both outside and in the kitchen. I loved mashing potatoes and eating them, and doing so sparked my

19

interest in cooking other things as well. I can remember helping her make butter with her butter churn and homemade cottage cheese with fresh milk from Grandpa's milk cows, Betsy and Maryanne. We also had fresh eggs for breakfast that I helped collect from the chicken house. I loved doing all these things with Grandma, but my biggest motivation was simply being around her. I also loved it because I felt needed, and she valued my help.

I had aunts and uncles who were five to ten years older than me, and they helped out too, but as the youngest one, I was Grandma's *little* helper. I never wanted to get in trouble because I didn't want to see her disappointed in me.

I felt like Grandma was my biggest fan, and she helped me feel confident. I held my head high because I could feel her love. She and her faith provided a strong foundation for me during the next few years as I made my way through elementary school.

Chapter Four

FITTING IN

I felt like I began to fit in in small ways and to gain the sense of normalcy I craved as I progressed in school. I was making it on my own for the most part and, thanks to Grandma's affirmation, I was beginning to have some real inner confidence. I didn't need to use Toni on the playground in familiar surroundings anymore after I was about nine or ten. But trust me, she was always there if I really needed to be extra bold and confident when I didn't genuinely feel that way. I especially used her when my confidence lagged in new social settings. I also still loved acting like her at home. I remember hoping I would be more like this confident character when I grew up.

It was during fifth grade when I finally started to feel like I could be part of the "in crowd." Some new girlfriends invited me to after school activities and sleepovers. Mom rarely let me have friends over to our house because it was extra work for her, and she never knew how she would feel.

I can remember when a newer friend, Jenny, said, "Come with me to my next 4-H meeting. I think you'll like it. We have fun and there's always snacks."

Toni jumped in acting, "You convinced me when you mentioned snacks. I'm excited to get started, and I would love to join the group." As a ten-year-old, I was glad Toni helped me because I was scared of what new people would think of me. My natural inclination, as Teresa, was to be very shy. Toni, however, was bold.

At 4-H, an organization usually associated with farming and agriculture but not tied to school, I learned cooking, sewing, and knitting. I also met a group of kids who were very kind to me. This smaller group brought out my confidence and less of a need for Toni. I could eventually be my true self, Teresa, with them.

These friends and doing activities I enjoyed were important to my emotional growth. I was also finally able to adjust to being the youngest in my class. I started to have the confidence to catch up with the other students. I was glad to be doing better than barely surviving in class like I had done previously. I had some ups and downs in junior high, like most kids do, but overall, I felt fairly normal.

Something else that helped my development was going to church with my family. As I mentioned in the last chapter, I went with my grandma when I stayed at her house. Grandma's church, where my dad grew up, was Church of Christ. I remember when that church had communion. They would pass the crackers plate and a cup of grape juice, and everyone drank from the same glass; I thought that was so gross. But, as I also shared, I loved Grandma's old traditional and small church. I also noticed how Grandma had always been active in her church.

Mom, and Dad followed suit being active in their own church, First Christian Church. My freshman year in high school my dad became a deacon there. In addition to going to church because my parents went, I liked going to that church because one of my good friends and her family were always there. I felt normal and part of the group and also soothed by worship music and prayers for the church as a community.

I got baptized in my parents' church. It was customary for high school students to profess their faith and be baptized by full immersion. My friends and I all got baptized around the same time. Every fall, our youth group also went on a hayride. We piled into a wagon with hay behind a tractor and drove to a farm somewhere to have a bonfire and s'mores.

At that church, we also had an annual 40-Hour Famine[4], an intentional time of fasting from food completely. Our youth leaders said this experience would help us to understand how those who are hungry feel. When we finally had dinner at the end of forty hours, we didn't eat just any meal, but a basic meal of white rice and green beans. Food never tasted so good, and the experience did help me understand how difficult hunger is.

Whether we were at the fire, sharing a meal, or getting through a fast, the youth group shared stories and our favorite Bible verses with each other. My favorite verse was Joshua 1:9 NIV, "Have I not commanded you? Be strong and courageous. Do not be afraid; do not be discouraged, for the Lord your God will be with you wherever you go." This verse remains one of my favorites as I write this book, decades later.

Perhaps church activities helped me feel like everything was fairly "normal" for the first three years of high school. I had good friends, I was a cheerleader, and had a boyfriend, Jay. He and I had a great time going to ballgames, movies, and just hanging out. Jay would sometimes come to church with me, and he knew that I wanted to wait until I got married to have sex. And he honored that.

Don't get me wrong, there were sometimes when we would drink alcohol with friends, and that brought up more temptations that were hard to combat. Being a teenager had many challenges with peer pressure. But we did our best to remain strong.

Though my high school years passed without too many problems, not all my memories of high school are good or fun. Being a teenager came with the normal push and pull with parents. Dad and I started to bicker more, and I thought I knew everything. I was trying to be my own person. I remember Mom and Dad repeatedly telling me the story about how I was born during a blizzard on December 19, 1961. The story always concluded with, *"You were born in a blizzard, and you've been that way ever since."* I'm not sure what they meant by that comment, but I took it to mean that I was difficult and unpredictable, like when a blizzard comes through.

Senior year was the hardest—especially the last semester. Classes were tougher. I turned seventeen in December that year. Jay was a year ahead of me and no longer at school. I had the stresses of thinking about college, ACT, and graduation.

I remember one particular day in the spring semester senior year like it was yesterday. It was a beautiful sunny day outside as I went up to the chalkboard. We were putting our writing assignments on the board, and the teacher would call us one at a time to go up. While I was at the chalkboard, someone said something. I can't even remember what they said, but it sent me into a tailspin.

Suddenly, I found myself slamming the chalk and eraser on the floor and yelled some response to the effect of, "Leave me alone, I'm doing the best I can." Everyone was staring at me. I left the room, thinking, *What just happened?* This kind of reaction was uncharacteristic of me.

I was embarrassed almost instantly. I was so upset. I was crying so hard, and I started to hyperventilate. I was wondering why I had reacted the way I did. I felt a little faint as I made my way to my dad's office. He worked at my school as a cooperative education teacher, helping students and their parents prepare for college and the workforce.

I was shaking all over, and my insides were shaking too. Immediately, I was lying in his office on the couch and curled up. I was there the rest of the day feeling nauseated and weak. I had no idea what was happening, and I wouldn't find out for years to come. After school, my dad carried me to his car and took me home. All I could do was rest and eventually sleep.

What had happened? The next day was awkward, but I survived. This pattern of losing control of my emotions, and reacting for some reason, continued. This kind of incident, as I would learn over time, would for many years be followed by sorrow and embarrassment that it had happened, as well as bewilderment about why it had happened.

One time, I was at a sleepover and was out of my comfort zone in a newer friend's house. I was scared to interact with her family and friends, but during that slumber party seemed like the perfect time to let Toni, my actress character, take over. I pretended that everything was okay and acted funny and charming around them. When I was trying to go to sleep that night, I played over and over in my head what went right and what went wrong. I asked myself, *How could I do better? What do these people expect of me?* That's what I wanted to give them. I once again, in a newer situation, felt more comfortable being Toni, who made it easier for me to be more confident around people I didn't know. I so wanted them to like me.

Because I had renewed success and it seemed easier in the moment using Toni, I continued my practice of turning to her. Then I would let myself lose it at home by crying, overthinking, and hoping to recover from the despair I felt.

I was upset between the dichotomy that was emerging. My natural self, Teresa, remained shy and unconfrontational; Toni, however, could backfire on me as she became abrupt and harsh, which was sometimes hurtful to others.

When I found out I hadn't been invited to something, and I saw those girls at school, I said, "I heard you girls had a fun time at Jenny's house, did you forget me? I like to have fun too." *That was not a good approach, nor was it nice,* I later thought.

Another time my girlfriends didn't react the way I hoped they would, Toni would again bark out harshly, "Why aren't you being nice to me. I try to be nice to you?"

Toni had a mind of her own, or maybe she was pulling bits of emotions that were deep inside me. I really didn't know who I was or what my emotions would do. *It had to be her when I snapped at people or got emotional,* I thought. *That isn't me.*

Although this front helped me through many tough social interactions, I desperately wanted to be my true self. But because of my fear of rejection, I felt I had to use Toni to bring confidence or to have difficult conversations.

All the while, I wondered, *Why can't I stop worrying about what others think and just be myself?*

I wanted to trust and believe my own abilities to handle difficult situations, but many times, I was my own worst enemy. Self-sabotage, in the form of my "charming" character, Toni, gave me, Teresa, low self-esteem. Somewhere in my mind, my mask confused my reality around people, and it added to my feelings of unworthiness. I saw myself as not good enough and my self-talk in my mind was often negative.

You're not interesting enough.

You're not smart enough.

Does anyone really love you? Does God?

Even though I believed in God, I lost my way senior year with the pressure of my emotions. I used Toni to be normal instead of being misunderstood and alone. To the outside world, Toni showed strength, confidence, and joy. Inside, though, I felt unseen and unloved. These were my own warped feelings, but I blamed God. This pattern of using her and then blaming God was turning into a repetitive cycle.

That last year of high school, I snapped at friends and family more, and I had to pause and ask myself,

What is going on?

Why did I react that way? I had no answers. I did, however, have regret. I had a gut feeling inside that something was wrong, but I didn't know what it was. It was like I had no control of my emotions anymore.

As graduation was approaching, not only was the stress of college ever-present, but my friends and I had to take action to preserve something that had been important to us. We had learned that unless some of us stepped up to be lifeguards, our town of Grant City, Missouri, might close our public swimming pool. So, two friends and I went to a nearby town at night to get our certification as WSI (water safety instructor).

My friends and I had many fun times at the pool through our junior high and high school years. Not only was it a great place to gather but when I was thirteen, I first found out that Jay liked me there. My friends huddled around me to spill the story of him talking about asking me out. The pool was a special place in my heart that fostered normalcy and easier, carefree days of my summers growing up. I didn't want it to close.

In addition to myself, three girls and one guy stepped up to be the manager and lifeguards of our local pool. I loved teaching swimming lessons and helping young children. A bonus of being a lifeguard was a great tan and blonder hair to start college. Looking good always boosted my self-esteem. During the summer, I would work all day, have a late dinner with Jay, and then head home to sleep. The next day was a complete Groundhog's Day.[5] Just like in the movie by the same name, nothing changed, and nothing was different from day to day. I liked (and still like) things to be the same all the time. I felt secure and safe having a routine.

After my relaxing summer working with my friends as a lifeguard at our local pool, I was getting ready to head off to college. I had enrolled in the college my dad went to, Northwest

Missouri State University, in Maryville, Missouri. I was excited to get out on my own and have freedom, but I was anxious about meeting new people. I also realized I was going to miss my family.

Tension had been somewhat high between my parents and me because I thought I knew everything, just like most teenagers do. Thank goodness, though, Mom's moods had gotten better during the last year. She was more level-headed than she had been during my earlier years of growing up. I think her pregnancy with my sister during my last year of high school really gave her a renewed purpose. Her being eight months pregnant at my high school graduation, was still embarrassing, though! My sister being born just before I would leave for college was a gift to her and our family. My brother was nearly ready for high school, and he was able to mostly take care of himself.

I was ready to take a new adventure by becoming my own boss, or so I thought.

I knew my life would change when I arrived at college, so the weekend before I started, I went to my ultimate place of comfort before my new life began—Grandma's house. I was ready to take a nap on her big bed after a meal of her comfort food. I didn't have a care in the world as I snuggled into Grandma's bed. I drifted off to sleep, forgetting the anticipation of uncertainty in my new season of life just ahead.

When I woke up, she asked me questions like, "Are you excited to go to college?"

Was I? "I suppose so," I said.

I loved being with her, but my mind started drifting off to all that I had to do to get ready for college.

Because I was getting anxious, my mind went to how I dealt with stress:

Would Toni be able to show up for me in college if I needed her?

Am I still going to have to be two people to be liked in college?

C hapter F ive

COPING IN COLLEGE

A s soon as I arrived at Northwest Missouri State University (NWMSU) in Maryville, Missouri, I knew I was where I wanted to be. Even though I had only moved forty miles away from my hometown of Grant City, I could tell that this experience was going to be different from high school.

I was hopeful that I would find normalcy in my new setting. The campus was very picturesque, and my dorm was on the older side of the campus, where the buildings were brick. They were the same buildings that were there when my dad attended the same school. I loved walking around the campus, which was full of various trees and flowers.

Not only was the campus aesthetically pleasing, but it also had an exciting energy as everyone arrived on campus and explored the dorm rooms. Mom came and brought my baby sister to move-in day, just as I asked. *Everyone loves babies, so having her would be a good icebreaker to help me meet people in my dorm*, I thought. Plus, I was really going to miss my baby sister—and I wanted just a little more time with her.

We went up to the second floor, where my room assignment was, and found my door. My name was written in beautiful calligraphy. My roommate wasn't there, but it was clear, she had already chosen her side of the room because the bedding and décor was in place. I would have liked to be included in the decision, but I settled in to my side of the room without much more thought about the matter.

I did, however, think, *Wow, this room is small. But it's my home now, so I need to get used to it. Everyone seems friendly and helpful. Maybe I can do this.*

Underneath the newness and excitement, I was experiencing an underlying sense of dread about what this first semester would be like. I finally met my roommate; she was quiet and had her boyfriend with her all the time. He lived off campus, and she would go to his place, so she was rarely in our room. However, I did find a friend from my home town, who was a year ahead of me, right across the hall. Finding her and her roommate helped me make many more friends.

My anxiety and fear of the unknown were ever-present. My good days were euphoric and unnatural at times, which I loved because I had great energy. It was fun at first. However, the dark side of me didn't stay quiet. I rapidly cycled like Jekyll and Hyde. My anger was fueled by some unknown fire inside me that I couldn't control. I could feel my depression dragging me down. Rather than cry uncontrollably, I found that my favorite place to be in those times at college was being in bed.

When I would go to sleep in my dorm room, I tried to think of the comfort of my grandma's bed, where nothing could hurt me. I didn't, however, find the same kind of rest in my dorm room bed. There was also so much activity in my dreams; sometimes I could even fly over places and watch what everyone was doing. I would wake up not really feeling rested, but I liked that sleeping was a time that I didn't have to feel unless my dreams got too intense or scary. There have even been times in my life when I woke up and couldn't decide if what I dreamt was real or a dream. My emotions didn't seem "normal." I was sometimes up and other times down. I never knew which it would be from one minute to the next. I wondered, *Is this how all young adults are?* I wasn't sure. I also questioned, *Are these mood swings normal?*

Instead of the excitement and fun I was hoping for, starting college was overwhelming with having a roommate, choosing a major, finding classes, meeting people, and finishing homework. I was still somewhat uncertain about what I wanted to be when I grew up. Because I had worked in a newspaper office at sixteen, I thought journalism or broadcasting might be a fit for me. I was excited to start. I started out being a broadcasting major with a French minor. I loved journalism in high school, so I thought, *Why not do broadcasting and put myself out there? I could act my way through it with Toni. It might be fun.*

I discovered in my first broadcasting class during my first year of college that I was not comfortable on the radio or on television. I kept trying, though, because I loved the energy of the people who were in my major.

Using Toni's persona allowed me to put on a show anytime I was around crowds of people—whether in my coursework or in my social life. Others never knew the anxious feelings I had welling up in me that Toni would help me hide. I would essentially apply the mask with Toni, who had it all together and loved being a fun person at dorm activities and in class. It was draining, however, to fake happiness.

When someone said, "How are you doing?"

I (or Toni) would say, "Great"—even though I didn't feel that way inside.

I convinced myself that was the response people really wanted to hear, and I wouldn't dare disappoint them. Hidden beneath the veneer, however, sadness and weariness began to build up—just like it had first done at a slumber party with new friends a few years earlier.

Toni would help me make it through each week, and then I would drive forty miles home to see my baby sister and Jay. Seeing them provided comfort and familiarity, which helped me prepare for the next week. I had to get through—one week at a time—and then I got rewarded by being "normal" Teresa with those I loved. The trade-off seemed to be working to enable me to keep going, and it helped that my family and Jay back home missed me too.

Jay had actually proposed to me out of the blue after my first week of college. He had planned it all out with his sister, who lived in Kansas City, just a few hours from my school. He asked me to come to the mall and then walked me into a jewelry store counter, where he talked to the clerk. He asked for the ring he had already picked out for me, turned to me, and casually asked me to marry him.

I was so surprised, and not in the way I had hoped for. Getting engaged was such an important time that I had looked forward to my entire life, but the way it played out in the mall wasn't anything like I had hoped. I imagined a dinner and the man getting on one knee to ask for my hand. But it was different. Instead of a romantic proposal, there was no special atmosphere or sentimental place arranged for us to be. It felt quick and transactional. It seemed more like he did it to take me off the market, but I pretended to be happy in the shock of the moment.

I don't even know what I said if anything for a minute or two. We had dated four years, so it shouldn't have been a surprise. I, however, was just starting college, and I was not thinking about marriage!

I did say yes, though. I was like a deer in the headlights standing in the jewelry store completely overwhelmed by what had just happened. I didn't know what else to do. I knew I loved him. I just wish I had been able to prepare. I wish Toni could have helped me, but even she couldn't speak for me in that situation. After I said yes, we went to his sister's house, where there was champagne. It all happened so fast.

Jay had been planning to stay in our hometown to work and make money. He wasn't on the college path—yet. He was back home during my entire first year of college, and I was away on campus. I started behaving in ways that were far from normal, which I had never considered before.

I became infatuated with a boy from my broadcasting class, and I began seeing him on the side. His name was Matt. He had auburn wavy hair and the prettiest brown eyes. He was made for the camera.

My connection with Matt had started over a joint class project. Then study sessions. Then one night, it happened—a kiss. And that was only the beginning.

As I thought back, the guilt hit me hard. Not just because I had betrayed Jay, but because I didn't know *why* I had done it. *Was it loneliness? Was it a real connection? Was I trying to destroy something good before it had a chance to hurt me?*

I knew I didn't need more chaos, but I wasn't being rational.

As my freshman year went on, I became even more interested —or maybe even infatuated—with Matt. On top of being handsome, he was very funny. I was thrilled that he liked me so much, but I was engaged. The ring on my finger was like a big stay-away sign to most guys. Matt and I were in many classes together. He knew I was taken, but he didn't care.

I continued to maintain both relationships. I saw Matt during the week, and I spent time with Jay on the weekends. I don't really know why I did it. I guess I loved the attention. I knew that it was wrong, and I felt guilty while I was with Matt because of the fact that I was engaged. Somehow though, I compartmentalized my time with each man and rationalized it in my mind. I had become very impulsive.

What was wrong with me? I was ashamed and confused. I don't know if I felt trapped after being engaged, or if I just couldn't think clearly anymore. I knew I couldn't keep running in circles, and after all that had happened, the weight of my choices began to hit me.

With such division in my heart, it started to be a constant struggle to manage my emotions, my time, and my study habits.

Even though I knew my personal life was a mess, I was either academically savvy enough, somehow driven enough, or somehow blessed enough to still get my work done. The manner in which I did it, though, was far from ideal. I would get up in the middle of the night to do my school work, which may not be abnormal for college students.

Soon, the hours when no one else was awake became my normal go-to time to get my work done. I could be heard typing my papers on an electric typewriter in the study lounge at all hours of the night because of my rollercoaster sleep patterns. Keeping these hours, along with my inconsistent personality and moods, which changed on a dime, sometimes made people question my methods and intentions. Some people in my dorm thought I was irresponsible, even though I was getting decent grades.

I was still able to function in spite of my mood swings. I also faced procrastination and sometimes had trouble allowing enough time to complete tasks. But I was somehow making it work well enough.

I remember early on in college I would go into a friend's room to be around someone. I just didn't want to be in my room alone. So, I would lie down on my friend's bed when there was a couple of other people in there, and the reassuring sound of friends talking put me to sleep. They would wake me up later when it was time to go to the cafeteria to eat. I'm sure at that time no one knew what was going on with me—including me.

Why was my internal clock so different from everyone else's?

During my time at college, I often reflected back to that incident in high school when my whole world changed in an instant at the chalkboard. My world was never the same after that day. Since then, my emotions had seemed out of my control. I can't even really describe how that incident impacted me.

I understood enough to know that I was flying by the seat of my pants. My erratic behavior surprised me because I'd always been very responsible and cared deeply about doing what was right. However, I started making bad decisions more often—on top of keeping up two relationships. For example, I would skip my part-time work study job at the desk in my dorm on campus to go to hang out with friends. My priorities were backwards. The worst part was that I didn't care about the consequences anymore. I would realize later that skipping work was a bad decision and have regret.

In my attempt to move forward with my emotions, I was functioning in the most dysfunctional way ever. My emotions continued to be up and down like a rollercoaster. However, there were also times when things went as planned—and in those times, I felt normal.

It seemed like those ups and downs had a mind of their own. I got through the year by looking forward to a less stressful time coming up when I would go home during the summer to lifeguarding at the pool, where I knew the routine. I was looking forward to strengthening my friendships from high school and especially to spend time with Jay and focus on just having one relationship without the distractions at school. I knew that I owed it to Jay to work harder on us, and I frankly needed to feel more settled myself, He gave me that stability. We definitely had a good summer together when I remained focused and didn't get distracted.

Despite having that steady summer season with Jay, I still didn't know what I wanted to do with the rest of my life. I didn't see Matt during the summer, but I knew I would have classes with him again in the fall. I did miss him. He had made me a tape of James Taylor's music that I listened to often. It was sometimes hard to be out of touch with him, but it was probably for the best. We had no texting then, and long-distance phone calls were expensive.

After I returned to school for my sophomore year, Matt and I once again had many classes together, and our chemistry brought us back together quickly. I did realize as the semester went on that he was kind of a ladies man who flirted with other girls. I had no claim on him; I was still engaged, so what could I do? This two-timing dating was getting more complicated, but at least by further into the semester, my schedule and routine was more set.

However, after the semester was over, things would change and be completely different. A change in schedule was very disruptive for me. When the semester changed, it didn't seem to be a complete disruption for others, but my emotions and lack of routine had sent me into a tail spin. I hoped to slow down and be settled, but I did not yet feel that way at all.

Thoughts of suicide began to surface spring semester of my sophomore year. I had decided to quit school. I packed my suitcase and drove home forty miles at about 12:30 a.m. I was done! I was crying inconsolably while I drove.

As I drove innocently along the road alone, an overwhelming feeling would hit me. Something in my head kept telling me, *Just drive off the road—it will make things better.* I fought that feeling with every fiber of my being and with a desperate prayer, I cried out, "Don't let my spirit break, be with me and help me!" I knew that as long as my spirit did not break, there was hope.

I was glad that by the time I got home, thankfully, I had begun to come to my senses. I stayed home for the weekend and put those bad thoughts out of my head. My prayer for help had strengthened my soul. I wish I had known that seasonal changes and changes in routine can affect college students in bad ways if they have mental health issues.

That spring, Matt and I once again had almost all of our broadcasting classes together, and we still enjoyed spending time together. I knew I was smitten with him, and I looked forward to seeing him because it gave me a boost in my spirit. His personality was so fun-loving.

We would have make out sessions in my room or his. I even went to the clinic on campus to start on birth control pills because our emotions were very strong, and I wanted to be prepared in case something happened. As I have mentioned, sex before marriage was against my beliefs, but I also recognized that I was becoming increasingly impulsive.

Near the end of my sophomore year, I was also considering breaking up with Jay. He was at home and not with me at school. If we were to stay together, I thought Jay needed to come to college with me. Also, people from my hometown who attended my college noticed that I was with Matt often at school. I knew I had to tell Jay, or they would. I had this war inside: *I loved Jay; so what in the world was I doing?*

I knew if I had any chance of making things right with Jay, I had to tell him the truth.

We were driving around, and I asked him to stop. I told him I had something I needed to tell him.

"I've been cheating on you at school," I said finally, my voice trembling. "With someone from class. I stopped talking to him, but I need to drop the classes we have together and not see him again. I know that now. I'm sorry I let it go so long, I wasn't thinking clearly."

Jay looked down. He was silent.

I couldn't read him, and that scared me.

He finally spoke: "Why are you telling me now?"

"Because I don't want to lie to you anymore," I said, tears slipping down my cheek. "And because I want to try again. Because I love you."

He was quiet again, then nodded slowly. "I don't know if I can forget it. But I can tell you're trying. And maybe that's worth something."

While Jay and I were in the car having this discussion about what I had allowed to happen with Matt, the song, "Torn Between Two Lovers" came on the radio. *Doesn't that just sum it up?* I thought.

After our discussion, Jay and I decided to stay together. So, I changed my major away from broadcasting to get away from

Matt. My advisor helped me figure things out so I could still graduate on time. I made it a priority to keep my word to Jay and became determined to find a new path of study.

My advisor told me with my current credits I could change to an education major. I chose a major in speech and theatre and a minor in English for secondary education. I could still use all my credits from broadcasting and graduate on time. So, I did that. *Did I want to be a teacher?* I wasn't sure, but I knew I needed to do something to no longer have this two-timing dating life.

As I worked to make things right in my personal life, I longed for the more "normal" days of my early high school years when all I had to worry about was spending time with friends and going to church. It was when things were simple and uncomplicated. But, I knew I had to adjust and deal with my current situation. Jay was mad that I had cheated on him, and I would need to focus on building trust again in our relationship.

I finished my sophomore year and then went back home for another summer at the pool and seeing Jay after work. The summer once again flew by.

Jay decided to start his own college career to be with me. I guess he felt that was the only way it would work for me with my crazy emotions and erratic behavior. He was a year ahead of me in school. Jay had gone to a vocational tech school in Missouri for auto body repair for two years after he graduated high school and had become very good at it. He even won competitions in his field. He loved his hands-on work, but he knew he wanted to be with me at school. He then enrolled in business classes.

I became a little more stable my junior year with him there to hold me accountable and to be by my side. That year, I managed to keep my fiancé, my grades, and get a job as a Resident Assistant (RA). I loved those aspects of my life because they gave me structure, and at that point, structure was my friend.

I also still loved weekends when I would take a break from school and go to my grandma's house. Many times Jay would go with me to dinner at Grandma's, and he and my dad would go hunting or fishing. While they were gone, I would sneak in a nap in Grandma's bed. As I mentioned earlier, I was always at peace there—no one could touch or bother me as long as I was in that bed.

I also loved going home to see my family and especially my baby sister when I wasn't on weekend duty for my RA job. My family and I would go to church where everyone knew me. That was something I looked forward to.

During my time as an RA, which spanned from the beginning of my junior year until I graduated from college, the girls on my floor named me "Mom." I was "Mother Teresa" to some. Having this job as an RA not only gave me purpose but it also helped me immensely because with the job came a private room. This detail may seem small, but I no longer had the stress of a roommate and sharing a bathroom. I loved the solitude and comfort of knowing I could shut my door and be alone at night to recharge.

Even though I appreciated the new solitude that was possible with having my own room, I enjoyed getting to know the girls on my floor who I served as an RA. Being a support for others was an extra perk because not only was I helping them but also I liked to be needed. It was a motivation to be part of something bigger than myself. I craved positive reinforcement. I had become friends with the other RAs on campus, which also boosted my confidence.

Part of this desire for affirmation from others was because I was beginning to develop some resentment toward Jay, who didn't understand what I was going through. I would cry at inopportune times.

He started saying something that he began to repeat. "I suppose you are going to cry again."

I explained that I was really hurt and that I couldn't contain my emotions. *Why didn't he understand that?*

He said it more and more—and his face said it when his words didn't. His words and thoughts were like daggers to my heart.

"Why are you being so mean? I can't help it when I'm sad," I said.

"Why are you so sad? You are too sensitive; you need to get tougher skin."

I loved him, and he loved me, so why was he being so harsh?

I found myself not only hurt by him every time this happened, but I was frustrated because I felt I had no control over my own emotions.

Maybe I should pull out Toni—she always knew what to do.

Toni was starting to be more aggressive than charming, like she used to be. I started saying exactly what I was thinking when I used her. Through me, she said, "Stop nagging me, I can cry if I want to. Why does it bother you so much?"

I knew this defensiveness wasn't the best approach. I tended to use Toni to defend myself. When I got a harsh reaction in return, I would settle into Teresa and cry and hyperventilate. Looking back, I think I was having a panic attack, although I didn't know that terminology at the time.

When I was using Toni, I would sometimes say overly harsh comments back or even curse out of the blue. I could get intense in this defensive mode and then have regret.

I think that is why I would go back to Teresa's voice and always say, "I'm sorry."

Toni could be rough on others, or at least I thought it was her.

I began to see that I was finding ways to hurt someone else before they hurt me. I never wanted to be hurt, so sometimes I would cancel on someone if I thought they might cancel an outing on me. Not having expectations helped if plans didn't work out.

A friend would say, "Do you want to come over and hang out or go to the movies?"

Not knowing who else would be there, or if I would get disappointed or say something that would hurt a friendship, I hesitated. Even though part of me wanted to go, I would say, "No, I'm busy, maybe some other time."

I reasoned, *I couldn't do anything wrong if I wasn't there.* But later, I felt left out because I didn't choose to go. This is just one example of when I sabotaged what I wanted for no good reason. *I should have used Toni and gone with friends*, I thought. *Next time I will.*

As I look back on these times, I wish that I would have understood that the hurts in my life needed healing and Jesus. I believed that Jesus was the Son of God, but I didn't know how to seek His help with the real issues in my life. I have, ever since I can remember, had a tendency to push bad experiences down deep inside of me instead of dealing with them. I also know that in hindsight, I started and continued self-sabotaging behavior like giving up before I tried, and then I would wonder why I failed.

I was my own worst enemy, and somewhere deep down, I guess I thought if I could control the hurt it might be easier to endure. Still, as I got ready to make another life transition into the work world, I was hoping that a life change would somehow help jumpstart a brighter future.

Chapter Six

NAVIGATING "THE REAL WORLD"

I graduated from college as planned with a major in speech and theatre. I had hoped I would find normalcy in the "real world." I soon found out, though, that even though my circumstances changed, my ability to manage life's challenges had not.

My first job, like times at college, was more than I could handle. I accepted a teaching job in a small school as an English and Speech teacher. My position was also responsible for the newspaper, yearbook, and the play. I was barely twenty-one. I think many times I was still that scared little girl, not knowing what I was doing, but afraid to say so. I had students who were eighteen, just a few years younger than me. It was bizarre—and way too much work.

I was not at all ready for the stress of that new job, my own apartment, and all the responsibilities that went with life. I was struggling with what my life would look like and trying to keep my head above water. The job consumed my life and my health, both physically and mentally.

And just like in college, I had a deep desire to be needed. That desire, as I'll explain, would get me into trouble. My mom often said I scared her because I would jump feet first to do anything. My go-to answer was usually "Yes, I'm in," or "I should try that." I recklessly moved forward. I guess I thought I was invincible at times. It may have seemed that I was fearless, but under the surface, I was afraid of everything that came with, "You're on your own." I once again was living a "fake it till you make it" lifestyle, using Toni, yet again. In my soul, I was still a little girl—naïve, shy, and scared.

My fear was especially real because of the emotional changes that I began noticing in high school and college. I felt like I was on an emotional roller coaster, which I attributed to being in a new environment with so many people. When I was in what I later learned was a manic state, I experienced an elevated mood and an increased, unnatural energy level. During those times, I knew no fear or boundaries. I was able to pretend that I was okay and that I knew what I was doing.

I knew that people had thought of me as sweet and nice, and I didn't want the impression that others had of me or that I had of myself to go away, even though many times my thoughts and actions as a working adult didn't reflect that happy person.

When my thoughts didn't meet their impressions, I remember thinking: *What is going on? Is this what it is like to be in the big place they call "the real world?"* I was either like Tigger, from Winnie the Pooh, who I loved—happy and jumping around, or I was like Eeyore—gloom and doom, and sleeping all the time.

It must be my workload and new surroundings, I thought. I was always looking for the "why" of my behavior, but I kept my questions mostly to myself, though I'm sure my emotions didn't go unnoticed by others. I just knew I wanted to appear normal—whatever that was.

I remember thinking, *I don't have time for a man in my life anymore*. I was busy with my new job and school activities, which frankly wore me out. I decided to break off my engagement with Jay without any notice. My rational reasoning was out the window. My decision was devastating to Jay, but at that time, my emotions had been up and down so much that I was numb to real, lasting emotions. I was barely surviving.

It didn't help that my dad was not happy with me either. For my entire life, he had dealt with my mom's emotions, which we later learned were mostly on the depressive side of bipolar. With my breakup, he believed I was acting out in an unreasonable way.

I doubt that he even remembers saying this, but he was angry and said, "You're a bitch, and no one will ever marry you."

That comment left a huge mark on me, and it stayed with me for many years because I really looked up to him.

Wow, I am a really bad person, I thought, brokenhearted because of what he had said.

My sad feelings took me back to when I was a child, when I remembered him saying, "If you're going to cry, I'll give you something to cry about."

I felt like he did give me something to cry about with those words. His anger and impatience were so hurtful. My heart ached.

Because of my dad's words, being unable to maintain a relationship with Jay, and ongoing conflicts with coworkers, I thought that I had unknowingly turned my world upside down. *Who was I now?* I wondered.

I didn't even recognize myself when I looked in the mirror. The next few years continued with ongoing feelings of unworthiness coupled with much drama and trauma. I didn't want to be out of control and unpredictable, but I was.

The only thing I believed I could control at the time was my diet, which consisted of a lunch that was barely anything. I went from a size twelve to a size two. I had a doctor tell me if I didn't start gaining weight, he was going to hospitalize me. I was becoming a burden to my own body, and once again, just like the first time it happened close to the end of my second year of college, suicidal thoughts came into my head. The thoughts, anxiety, and stress just kept coming. I lost so much weight that in March 1984, before I finished my school year as a teacher, the doctor put me in the hospital for three days to be evaluated.

My desperation for acceptance from others continued after I was released from the hospital and gradually contributed to me getting involved in unhealthy situations. For example, I started supporting a friend financially because it made me feel important. I could barely take care of myself, but I had told her grandparents that I would help her out. I really didn't have the extra money to spare so the right answer at that time would have been "No, I am unable to take on her responsibility." Hindsight is 20/20. But at that age, in the moment, I allowed myself to take on burdens that weren't mine, and I tried to fix things for others. I would say, "yes" to things just to feel significant.

At one point, I met a guy who I knew was not good for me. Other people tried to tell me that, too. I knew I was making a mistake, but my reasonable mind had left the building. The relationship was abusive and manipulative from the beginning, which made my emotions flare in response. My moods were beyond my control, which only made the situation worse during the six months that I was with him. I had a hard time looking out for my own interests, so the relationship continued.

I wasn't rational when I was triggered in that relationship. One time, I got angry and ran full force into a glass door with my head, breaking the glass. I ended up with barely a scratch, but looking back, it could have been so much worse.

During another instance with this guy, I was crying hysterically because I was hurt, and my emotions were intensified ten times or more. I took off in my car, sobbing and hysterical. I went to the highway and put the pedal to the metal. I got up to over 100 miles per hour. Then I slammed on the brakes, and the car spun around. It stopped, and I wasn't hurt. I knew then that Jesus had the wheel and had protected me.

During another situation with this guy, when we were arguing by his car, I ended up falling and hitting my head on the pavement. I suffered a concussion and a skull fracture and ended up in the hospital. I had to be log rolled every few hours by the nurses because of the risk to my brain. These injuries are just three of the many that could have harmed or even killed me. My concussion was a wake-up call that I needed to end this relationship—we had always been like oil and water. So with a friend's help, I did end it. *Thank God.*

I felt like I had no control over my actions, and at times, it was as if I was having an out-of-body experience. Even though I was unaware of what I was doing in the middle of the incident, I could replay it in my mind afterward. As I recounted what happened, regret would build, especially when I was unkind or would snap at others. I knew after the fact that these responses weren't the way God wanted me to act. He rescued me so many times that after every incident, I thought, *God must want me alive for a pretty good reason to keep sparing my life!* I kept telling myself that, anyway. Whether or not I believed that thought depended on the day.

With all the unhealthy situations I just shared, I had become exhausted physically and mentally. In addition to being anorexic, the doctor said I had "please others drive." It is an actual condition in psychology that I'd never heard of.

Regardless, he recommended that I try to care for myself more and to find more balance in my life by simplifying it.

Before I followed his advice and got help, I was like a leaf blowing in the wind, not knowing where I would land or what kind of mood I would wake up with. For example, I would have way too much energy some nights and stay up late, which made the next day a struggle. And, if I let my feelings take over and didn't feel like paying attention to disciplines that I knew were good like eating right, exercising, and quiet prayer time, they became nonexistent. Just like I had been since I had to choose a major, I was still asking myself, *What is my purpose in life?*

In an effort to find that purpose and find the ever-elusive normal I craved, I sought a different career. I thought that changing my work situation would improve my life. I knew pretty quickly that teaching wasn't for me. So, after one year in that profession, I found a different job in a new town and moved. I hoped to make the best of a new start.

So, in September 1984, when I was 22 years old, I began working at Graceland College in Lamoni, Iowa. This was the job I mentioned earlier in the book. My affinity for journalism had continued in college, even though broadcast journalism hadn't been quite the right fit.

My pride wanted positive affirmation for everything that I did, so I was glad to be working on publication projects for Graceland. It wasn't what I had trained for, but my new job allowed me to have ideas and produce pieces that others read and liked. I loved my creative side and being around creative people. Eventually, I worked up to be the assistant manager of the college's publication center. Even though my life was better than the year before because I loved my job, my personal life was still a mess.

After two years of being in Lamoni, I became sad looking back on my personal life. I had moved and been focused on my profession. I had dated some, but, because I wanted to do better than before, I hadn't gotten close to anyone who was good for me. I realized that if I had the fortitude to make things work with Jay, I might have been married for at least two years already.

Around the time I was lamenting my past, in January 1986, by chance or God, I met Adam. As I shared earlier, he was still a student at the college where I worked, he was my age. We started doing things together and enjoying each other's company. He introduced me to many of his friends who were athletes, and I introduced him to my friends as well. I developed healthier friendships and was starting to feel a part of the community in town. I was trying to become physically healthier by exercising, eating better, and lifting weights. I was getting stronger, but I also had burdens that I couldn't shake from emotions that, at times, made no sense.

Once again, I started increasingly having more times when my feelings ran wild, so it seemed, for no reason. I had a good job, a boyfriend, and other friends, but at times, the utter despair that I felt when I was alone was more than I could bear. But as I said, I tried to fake it till I made it every day. Some days were better than others, and I loved the excitement when I was in what I now know is a manic state. I was euphoric and unstoppable. And I had no fear. I was game for anything, and I loved feeling that way. More times than not, however, that feeling was followed almost like clockwork with a trip to the pit of despair. I hated that place. It was lonely, inconsolable, and scary.

As I mentioned, I had thoughts of ending my life my sophomore year in college, when I was nineteen years old. Those thoughts crept into my mind at times, and especially when I lived in Lamoni in my mid-twenties. I was still trying to look back and find good memories in the midst of the bad. But I had an even harder time looking forward with hope. There had already been so many ups and downs and, once again, I was feeling down and hopeless more often. I could barely get myself out of bed many times. I didn't even want to.

Though I had good times with Adam and my friends, there was a weightiness to my emotions that I didn't understand. The thoughts of being done with life entered my head more and more in 1986 until that December day when I was almost twenty-five and tried to end my life right before my birthday. God led me in His own way to a place where I could get help—in the hospital with a diagnosis I never wanted—bipolar disorder.

Although I didn't realize it at the time, having a name for what was happening in my mind turned out to be a blessing in disguise. I know the suicidal thoughts would have continued without that diagnosis and the help that was available once my condition had a label.

I had faced a long road leading up to my suicide attempt and diagnosis. As I was lying in the hospital bed, I wished I could have gotten those years back, but I couldn't. I still wanted to try to understand more about why my life had been riddled with unexplained ups and downs, and I was ready to do whatever I could to have a different outcome moving forward. I was told that I could look for warning signs to help me ward off future episodes. As time went on, I gradually was able to see the signs more clearly and I would also, over time, learn strategies to help me prevent disaster.

My first priority, though, was to move forward and to make a new start.

C hapter S even

God Forging a Different Path

In February 1987, after we had dated for a little over a year, as I mentioned, Adam and I broke up on amiable terms. I was getting help for my bipolar in the form of medication and family counseling at the time, as I also shared. I was working on accepting all that had happened leading up to my suicide and its aftermath. I wondered what the future would hold, and as I continued to understand more about my illness and that there were ways to deal with it, I became hopeful and determined again. I had adopted some new techniques to feel more relaxed and settled. I knew I needed to be more intentional about rest and other healthy habits. I also began looking for more ways to keep my moods level as I tried to rely on God more.

In fact, I even thought, *As I see new doors or opportunities open up, God willing, I will step through them.*

A door from God can be a simple nudge that feels right in the soul. I was also aware that there are doors to the past that were definitely not from Him.

By July 1987, I had been praying for a change for a few months. I was sensing it was the end of my time at Graceland College, and once again, after three years in the same place, I had a nudge to start over. I was convinced after my suicide attempt that getting away was truly the best route to take. I wanted to shut doors from my past. I thought it was best to refuse to revisit old memories, so I pushed them down, but I knew they were just below the surface.

In November 1987, I had been in contact for three months with a company that came to the publications center. This company that was interested in my skills came to Graceland, and I gave them a demonstration of the typesetting and computer equipment that I used, and that is when they offered me a job interview.

The company was in Orange City, Iowa, more than 300 miles away from anyone I knew, but I believed that God had made this path for me. Maybe it was for the job, maybe it was simply for a fresh start, or maybe it was to meet new people. I had to at least go and see what might be in store.

The idea of changing my life by stepping into this new position was exciting and scary all at the same time. My interview went well, and I liked the way the large white corporate building sat amid cornfields. Even though I had been previously looking for work in Kansas City, a city of more than one million people at the time, I was more of a small-town girl, and Orange City, with about 5,000 people, seemed like a better fit. The town had beautiful homes, and the people I had met during my interview process were very kind. I was excited about my future, and all the town had to offer.

The only problem was that I wasn't sure who I was yet. I wondered if I was trying to escape from the real problem—my emotions. *Wouldn't I just take them with me?* But, I had a Holy

Spirit nudge like a gut feeling that God would lead the way. I said yes to a change even though I was afraid.

I accepted the job and returned to Orange City with my mom, and we drove right to the house where my new boss lived. He knew my mom was coming with me, so he offered to show us around town and had some apartments lined up for us to look at. We met in person when he visited Lamoni a month earlier, and we had been in touch since then. We had professionally clicked. He was like my dad in personality, and about the same age. I could tell he was going to be a tough, straight-shooting boss, but I appreciated that and felt at ease.

As we drove up to his house, I admired it when I first saw it. It was a two-story Spanish-style stucco house. *I would be so happy to live in a house like that someday*, I thought. But I knew purchasing a home wasn't what would be best during that phase of my life. I had to get to know the area, get on a stronger foot financially, and be sure I wanted to stay in Orange City.

My mom and I took my boss up on his offer to have him take us around to various areas to assist me in looking for apartments. I fell in love with an apartment that had been converted from an old small church. The choir loft was the bedroom, and it looked over the living room and dining room below. It had great stained-glass windows, and wonderful light was always coming in. *How perfect*, I thought. *I am going to be living in God's house in a place where God led me.*

My moving boxes got there before I did because the company had a moving company bring all my belongings ahead of me. It was nice not to have the burden of carrying everything in myself.

It was easier to settle in than it had been with my previous move. And I loved my new place! It felt like home right away.

I knew God was with me too. I counted on that belief. After all, He had saved me—not only from a myriad of accidents and not smart situations, but even when I had tried to kill myself for a reason, and since that time, I had believed that it was my job to rely on Him and figure that reason out. I would have said I had a relationship with God since my baptism in high school, but because of residual shame, I had a hard time saying "God" out loud after I had sinned trying suicide. I usually referred to Him as, "The Big Guy Upstairs." I knew He was there, but I hadn't grasped fully that He loved me unconditionally despite my flaws and mistakes.

I was still uncertain where this new path and new job that I had chosen would lead me, but I wanted a new chance at "normal" as I started my new life nearly a year after my suicide attempt and my diagnosis. After I got settled as 1987 came to a close, the hard part came: making friends and starting life over in a new place. Though the idea of reinventing myself was exciting, it was also scary.

Sometimes, when I was in my apartment alone, I didn't know exactly why I had been brave enough to move, and I wondered if this decision would backfire. But then again, I had a tendency to wonder and worry whether my decisions were God or me. Though I had faith, many times fear would sneak in. I prayed and I trusted in my heart that the move had truly been God's leading—or if it hadn't, that He would make it work anyway.

I was determined to move forward with God's guidance. I had bought a plaque for my new apartment that read, "This is the day the Lord has made, don't mess it up." This piece of décor helped me remember to seek God's leading and not my own.

I was pleasantly surprised by my new work environment, which included graphic artists and publication designers. It was a promotional marketing company, and the artist produced logos for caps, embroidery, and screen prints. Advertising and page layout were also done for in-house projects, along with their own printing department. My job was to train the traditional artists to do their art on the computer. I loved creative people. They seemed to be very welcoming to those who were different, and at that time, I felt different.

I felt like my new job was becoming a great adventure. It was created just for me, so all I really had to do was what my boss asked of me to help propel the artists further in their future endeavors. I was a support system, which meant I was needed and did everything that I could to please them. This role and feeling significant was fulfilling. I tried to always be happy and cheerful. People could see my heart, and I always made sure they saw the best of me if I could help it.

There was plenty of stress and down times at work, but I tried to hold in my up and down feelings for the most part until I was home alone and could let my guard down. Some stresses, especially interacting with others who were also stressed, caused too much anxiety for me to contain my emotions. If I was feeling vulnerable at work, however, I could still retreat to my office. I could redirect my efforts to work on preparing for training or fixing computer hardware or software problems because the computer couldn't interact with me on an emotional level, and that was just what I needed to get past how I was feeling.

The other great part about working in a department of artists is that many of them were a little eccentric, and their behaviors weren't always picture-perfect. It was a place of fun and jokes. We had containers of Laffy Taffy, and we would read jokes that were printed on the inside of the wrapper almost daily. We did our best not to take everything super seriously, so it was usually a relaxed environment.

As I mentioned, I did my best to wrestle with any harmful moods that were bubbling up outside of work. I started to seek God more intentionally to level my mind. I tried to reduce the chaos in my mind by doing progressive relaxation that I learned a year earlier. *Just breathe and pray*, I would tell myself. I also tried to distract myself by spending time with friends. I did the best I could to contain or push down bad emotions. Sometimes I could contain my emotions, and other times, I couldn't. I hated when my emotions got out of control, so working on them was always a priority for me.

After I was there only a month or two, Adam, my ex-boyfriend who was with me during the time of my suicide attempt, called me. Adam and I still talked on the phone a little until one day he asked me to help a friend of his who was beginning to suffer from bipolar disorder.

He said, "She is going through some of the same moods and ups and downs that you were. Do you think you could help her walk through it?"

This idea scared me, and I knew I was not capable of helping anyone at the time. I could barely help myself, and out of fear, I said I didn't know, and I never called him back. We never spoke again. That decision was one I regretted, but at the time, it was all I could do. I was frozen in fear. Even to this day, I do not know what happened to either Adam or his friend.

Maybe in an effort to calm my guilt over not helping Adam's friend, I began to pray, "God please help me to help someone someday."

Within the first year of being in Orange City, perhaps because I wanted others to know more about me, or perhaps because I was getting more comfortable in my work environment, I started telling people that I had been diagnosed with bipolar. Maybe I shared my diagnosis because I also wanted them to know in case my emotions flared. I was protecting my new friendships by being totally honest, but I was still fairly new at managing the reality of living with bipolar.

I didn't scare anyone away, so that was good. When I told people outside of my immediate circle of friends and family, I began to realize that there was—and is—a stigma to this illness. I guess I was a little naïve.

Sometimes I felt like I was still putting up a front with Toni to protect people from some of my true emotions, or maybe I used her to not let people too far in to protect my heart. Looking back, I believe it was the latter. I continued to put up walls, all while functioning well and working hard.

The walls especially came up when I started dating again. I learned that when I opened my heart too far, I was asking for hurt in relationships. Maybe my dad had been right. His harsh words had been disturbing me since the day he had spoken them, and unfortunately, they would still somewhat affect me for years to come. They left an indelible mark, leading me to internalize feelings of unworthiness, self-doubt, and self-sabotage in the form of low self-esteem. I engaged in therapy to process these hurts, but engaging in forgiveness was easier said than done, and it was an ongoing process.

I also realized I was harboring hurt from my most significant relationships—Adam and Jay. I guess I thought I dealt with the hurt, but actually, I suppressed some of the memories.

I would often quote the phrase of Scarlet O'Hara in *Gone with the Wind*. "I can't think about it right now. If I do, I'll go crazy. I'll think about it tomorrow."[6] I would throw my problems to the wind. I would eventually learn the hard way that avoiding the processing of hurts was not the same as healing wounds. And spending time with new people at this time in my life was part of that avoidance. *Staying busy helps,* I thought.

For me, dating continued to be a rollercoaster. It was hard. If I liked someone, it seemed like they were terrible for me because they triggered my emotions or made me angry. Because I didn't feel confident in myself, I had developed a liking for boys who weren't emotionally available. Interactions with them turned into unhealthy and dysfunctional relationships because, at times, I started lying and was still pulling out Toni. I cried myself to sleep because I was trying to please someone, but I felt like I was being taken advantage of. If I liked someone, and he liked me back, I became nervous. I knew he didn't know all of me. *How could anyone else get to know the real me when I didn't even live out my true self after everything I had been through?*

If I got to know a man enough to feel comfortable, I would start to let my guard down. Somehow I could only date men who weren't trustworthy or honoring me. I ended up being hurt deeply as I gave my heart away too quickly to that type of guy again and again.

On the other hand, if a guy treated me well, I was bored with him, and I began to sabotage the relationship. This pattern of either choosing dysfunction or abandoning potentially healthy relationships out of fear and boredom went on for about four years in my mid-twenties.

I'll give you just one example of dating during that season of life. One boyfriend in Orange City, Ben, was a distraction, and not that different from others I had encountered since I moved. He was very much a perpetual bachelor, and I was not going to change his mind. In this small town, like others, it seemed the good ones were already taken by the time they were in their late twenties. I'm not sure why I got caught up in Ben's drama and settled for a non-marriage bound relationship when marriage was what I wanted. I guess it was fun for a while. But, at twenty-eight, I was ready for real and lasting love.

Drawing on Toni, I confronted Ben one night after months of dating, "I know I'm not easy. My mind gets loud; my heart gets heavy. Some days, I'm just trying to hold it together. And I thought…maybe if someone like you could love me, I'd finally be whole."

Ben responded, "That's a lot of pressure to put on someone."

65

"I know," I said. "And it's not your job to save me. But it's also not fair for you to keep showing up halfway—just enough to keep me hoping, never enough to stay."

"That's not fair. I like you, but I never promised you anything."

"True. You promised nothing—and I settled for that. I kept calling it love when really it was me trying not to scare you off. But I'm done shrinking to be lovable. I've done that before. I need more. And maybe you're not the one who can give it."

That would be the end of another relationship. I knew I needed to leave and not look back. Knowing what was best for me did not take away the sadness of another breakup though.

At least Toni helped me do the right thing by telling the truth that time. However, I was still disillusioned and downright discouraged with dating. I started thinking that being by myself was maybe the best option. A girl gets tired of dating with no good results.

Still, once the immediacy of the latest break-up passed, I still wanted more desperately than not to get married and have a family. But I wasn't sure that would happen for me. Despite my doubts, I still felt God had brought me to Orange City for a reason. I stayed, not knowing what the future would hold.

C hapter E ight

WONDERING WHAT WOULD COME NEXT

As I approached the end of my twenties, I was asked to be in my good friend Katherine's wedding. Our friendship blossomed after we were both featured as new employees of the month in our company's magazine shortly after we met four years earlier. I was Miss November, and she was Miss February. We had always been grateful for our jobs and how the company affirmed creativity, but we were both convinced we would both move on to spread our wings beyond our small town after a year or two—and yet, four years later, neither one of us had left.

I said yes to being in her ceremony, and of course, was very happy for her, as well as for my other friends who were getting married or expecting a baby. Sometimes, however, I felt like a third wheel. But I was grateful to be doing well at my job, and I felt more settled than I ever had in Orange City, so I decided to stay.

I wondered as I approached thirty if I would finally find that special someone. I was making good money, and except for a history of unhealthy relationships, I saw myself as pretty stable. I at least looked like I had it all together in public, which was important to me. I knew deep down that I was a good and happy person, and that is what I wanted people to see.

I still held on to relics of my past that helped me feel loved and safe. One of those items was a teddy bear Adam had given me six years earlier—the kind that wears a winter cap and scarf. This stuffed bear had become my confidant and snuggling buddy. It had made the move 300 miles away from my home state to Orange City. I could have filled a lake with the tears shed on that bear through the years. I had named him Joey, and he was my go-to companion in times of despair. I also relied on sleeping to escape, along with junk food. I used Mountain Dew to self-soothe. I had gotten in the habit of drinking Mountain Dew when I was in college because of my sleeping patterns then. I told myself I could have worse habits—and I still indulged in my habits of choice.

I was in the early stages of accepting that God made me just the way I was—warts and all. Acceptance can take years, and it did. I wasn't completely okay with the way God had made me. *I am flawed,* I thought. I often grumbled to Him about my shortcomings. Trusting and believing Him was difficult for a person like me. I had strong sensory feelings and was very empathetic, so pleasing others to ensure I was okay became a crutch. Portraying myself as normal and happy seemed to make my friends and coworkers happy. Therefore, I was still leaning on Toni somewhat. Here's just one of many conversations when Toni helped:

"Teresa, how's your day going?" friends would ask.

"I'm doing great," was my (Toni's) response even though many times I was barely surviving some days. I would exchange pleasantries, and *no one was the wiser,* I thought.

Looking back at how my emotions were so unpredictable, it seemed that there were times of merely surviving, and also other times when I began to tap into my deeper connection with God.

I also committed to going to church again and focused on turning my life around. I had learned from dating that some people deliberately pushed my buttons to try to get me to have a reaction. I decided that manipulative people no longer had a place in my life. I didn't want to deal with those types of antics anymore. I resolved not to date just to have someone. I believed God would not let me down in the long term if I protected myself from unhealthy relationships. So I avoided them by busying myself with church, church activities, and being with friends in social settings, along with focusing on my work.

Despite my best efforts to trust Him, some part of me had given up on my dream of marriage and a family. I was definitely discouraged. I felt I might become what was referred to as an "old maid" with my standards.

It wasn't that I didn't get attention from men or even genuine affection from them, but I always had an "I AM" hanging over my head, and I knew that was a big pill for someone else to swallow. The "I AM" that was hanging over my head was "I AM Bipolar." I struggled with my identity for many years before I finally changed my I AM from I AM bipolar to I AM a child of God and beloved with a bipolar diagnosis. The way we say things—even to ourselves—does matter. I'll explain how I learned to revamp my words later in the book; for now, suffice it to say, I wish I had internalized the truth of who God says I am earlier in life.

I won't lie—moving past twenty-nine had really hit me hard! I wondered, *What are my thirties going to bring? Will there ever be someone out there who gets me?* Still, I went into my next year—the beginning of my fifth year in Orange City—with a glimmer of hope and with prayers for my future.

I have learned that when we stop looking for what is next, God steps in. When we stop controlling, He offers to lead. I discovered this important lesson when I stopped controlling my dating life and surrendered, because that is when he brought Doug to me. God literally had Doug walk up with another friend when I was at Katherine's house. His athletic and handsome appearance struck me right away, and I wanted to get to know him.

For the previous five years in Orange City, I dated mainly to look like I was part of a couple during social events, and to cover up my pain. As soon as I saw Doug, however, I wondered if my situation would be different; Doug was divorced but nice. We began as friends, just having fun together. I told him all about myself, and over time, I became increasingly vulnerable—more than I had been in the past.

And as God works, I liked Doug more and more, and he wasn't scared away when I told him that I had a bipolar diagnosis. I was glad that he wasn't scared, but I was sure the relationship probably wouldn't last. *I would mess it up somehow*, I thought. The harsh words that my dad had said to me about not getting married still hadn't left, and as I have shared, they made me scared to even be in a healthy lasting relationship.

The fact that Doug and I had met at a mutual friends' home and that we had several friends in common was helpful. After we had been friends for a few months, I decided to ask him to come over for dinner. He said yes, and we had such a good time that he asked me out for his birthday two days later, February 4, for a movie and dinner. We began officially dating in early February 1992. We enjoyed our free time together.

In September 1992, Katherine, who was already married at that point, and I went on an adventure, a girl's trip, where I heard her talk about her hubby. She shared about how great it was to relax at home and just spend time together as a couple. She loved being settled and not dating anymore. I knew that I really wanted Doug to be my husband so we could be together all the time and share life.

A couple months passed after our girls trip. I didn't know that Doug had been saving for a ring. As usual, I got impatient and said through tears, "Are you going to marry me or what?"

Doug was quiet for a while. Then he took me by the hand and showed me his account. I saw, *He had been saving for a ring*.

He said, "I am sorry I've waited so long. I love you and want to marry you!"

I was then disappointed with myself and my lack of patience because that was a moment I couldn't get back. I had basically just asked him to get married. I could see the big picture of our lives together, and I wanted him to see it too. In retrospect, if I had simply brought up our future, maybe I would have gotten that proposal that I had always hoped for.

God, however, worked everything out. We went to Omaha shortly after that incident, and we picked out an engagement ring. That December, we began planning for an October 1993 wedding, when I would be thirty-two. Grandma always said that nothing that was good ever came easy. It takes work and commitment. *I will have a chance to apply this lesson in our engagement and in our marriage*, I thought.

Our friends had a couple's engagement shower for us, and Doug and I continued planning our wedding together. I have to admit, I was a little nervous because I never knew what my mood would be, but I was also excited about our plans. Everything was falling into place. My medication helped my moods for the most part, unless I was triggered, in a very stressful situation, or lacked sleep.

We focused on our wedding for ten months. Doug and I worked on it together, although he was fine with me making most of the decisions. I had always been a procrastinator, so the wedding seemed no different. I got the big things done right away, photographer, pastor, flowers, food, dress, etc. But the last few days before the wedding were hectic. I was making our rehearsal dinner myself, and my friends were serving it. I was welcoming people from out of town, and I didn't get my wedding program put together and printed till the night before we were married. I had my nails done and my hair put in an updo the morning of the wedding. As I look back, I am not sure how it all got put together at the end, but it turned out perfectly.

Our wedding took place on October 2, 1993, a picture-perfect fall day. The maple leaves by the church were turning into a brilliant display of red, yellow, and green, and the temperature was not too cold or hot. About 150 people—everyone we held dear—surrounded us. I was happy with my décor for the wedding, which was the Victorian look I wanted. My flowers and candles fit the theme too. I was thrilled with my ivory dress with its intricate beading and its off-the-shoulder mermaid style. My heart was so touched at how Doug cried when I reached him at the front of the church. He loved me, and I could see it on his face. He was perfect for me, and I loved him. What a beautiful day!

At the ceremony, everyone was in great spirits. Grandmas, grandpas, aunts, uncles, my mom, dad, brother, and sister had all travelled 300 miles to be there. I was also so grateful that I still had my dad to walk me down the aisle. We had our wedding at Trinity Church in Orange City, where we attended. The reception was at a golf course club house in Hull, a nearby town where Doug grew up. At our reception, we danced to, "Can I Have This Dance for the Rest of My Life" by Anne Murray, and we both meant it. The next day, we left for a beautiful honeymoon in Cancun, Mexico.

I believe that marriage is God's masterpiece in progress. The beginning is a blank canvas, and at first, all that is seen is something like a splash of brown on the canvas. If you saw it, you might think, like I did, *What a mess*. I know I didn't understand where the proverbial art—our lives—was going. But I chose to stick around because I knew so much more was to come. As I watched over time, seeing God, the artist, add more and more strokes, I started to see—and am still seeing as I write—a beautiful painting.

As God has created His masterpiece in my life, He has at times revealed His sense of humor and timing. Sometimes, as He works toward the beautiful, all I see is some ugly. I realized that some marriages don't survive the ugly—the "hurt and forgiveness"—phase. Marriage with or without bipolar isn't for the faint of heart. It takes work, commitment, constant nurturing, and attention. I learned these lessons the hard way. But I'm getting way ahead of myself. Let me go back and tell you about our early years of marriage.

Several months after Doug and I married, we began thinking about a family. My biological clock was ticking, and we didn't want to wait long. We continued to spend quality time with each other and our friends, and we both enjoyed our jobs. As we expected, there were hard days, but I think we both thought that we had "arrived" at our ideal jobs, and we both planned to stay where we were. We were doing well with two incomes, and we were talking about buying a home. We had intentionally planned to rent for the first year or so, but it was time for us to move forward with some major decisions, like buying a home and having children.

We looked at a small starter home. I was so glad that Doug and I were on the same page with timing. I had been praying to God about all these issues. God was so good, enabling us to purchase a great house that was just the right size to start our family.

74

As we settled into our new home, life felt good and full of promise. This sense of security gave Doug and I a nudge to grow deeper in our faith. The good thing was that Doug and I both came from a church background. We continued to attend the church where we were married. We both liked it, so we stayed there. It was a good beginning. I think there is a reason that God didn't—and still doesn't—want us to look too far into the future. I believe staying in the present helps us to be grateful for every stage He takes us through.

We had good intentions of creating unity as a new family, but in practicality, because Doug and I had both been on our own for a while, we both had our own way of doing things. And at our age, neither of us was overly willing to change. Our lack of flexibility could cause tension at times; my moods didn't help either. Doug was a firstborn child, just like me. We were both used to being in charge.

His family and the town where he grew up were both much like mine. We discovered both of us had been lifeguards during our summers and that our dads both liked sports and watching television. For as many differences as we had, we also had similarities. We both liked to golf, so that was an activity that we often did with friends.

Most of our friends had kids, so we decided to try for a baby after we had been married for a little more than a year. I would have to stop taking all the medication for bipolar leading up to and during my pregnancy. Doctors said my medications could affect fetal development and even cause birth defects. This news was scary because I wasn't sure how being without my meds would affect me emotionally, but I was committed to get off of it because I wanted a family.

A few months later, the home pregnancy test came back positive. As I expected, I experienced difficulties at times at home because without my medication, I could get very emotional. Plus, my hormones were changing. I got angry and cried more frequently than I would have liked, but Doug and I also understood that emotions are heightened for most pregnant women.

Nine months later, on July 27, 1995, Doug and I welcomed our first child, a boy, Cooper Lee. Because I had a C-section, he had a perfectly round head. I thought he was so beautiful. Everyone commented on what a handsome boy he was. Also with the C-section, I had to recover for several hours, so I was lying there while Doug got to go with the nurse to see Cooper weighed, measured, and scored on the Apgar test. He was eight pounds, seven ounces, and twenty-one inches long. Although I couldn't feel my legs because of the epidural, I thanked God that there were no problems.

Chapter Nine

CARING FOR BABY COOPER

I wanted to do everything right for our perfect baby, Cooper Lee. I was determined that I would be a better parent than my parents, but isn't that the way we all feel? We think we are smarter, and we want to learn from the mistakes they made with us. To that end, I had read the books, *What to Expect When You're Expecting, What to Expect the First Year,* and *What to Expect the Toddler Years.*[7] I thought that I was on top of this child-raising thing. I would soon discover how different life would be from my expectations.

We didn't know for the first year or two that anything was off; after all, we were new parents, and whatever our son did was amazing. To us, it was okay that he didn't meet every milestone in the books; he was so smart and was growing into the cutest blonde-haired, blue-eyed boy. As he started to walk, he was everywhere. He got into the cabinets, so the house had to be childproofed. He was fast. I chalked this up to him being a boy and having a strong curiosity.

Looking at him, I saw that he fit right into the Dutch community that we lived in because he was so blonde and looked like many of the other kids. He didn't, however, act the same. I began thinking that he might be struggling with Attention Deficit Hyperactivity Disorder (ADHD).

As he began to talk and socialize with other kids at the park, I noticed that he was very persistent in staying close to them, telling them who he was, and wanting to play with them. He was increasingly persistent. It was to the point that other kids shied away from him, and parents would leave the playground because he was too friendly and would cling to the kids. I thought, *I feel bad for him; he just wants to make friends, but he doesn't know how.*

Cooper had been at daycare since he was only a few months old. His daycare provider, Lisa, was amazing with him. She kept him at her home with her own boys. She was trained in early childhood development, and she had even ran a preschool in the past. She noticed things about Cooper that were emerging, like other kids she had seen with special needs. I reasoned that *maybe Cooper was just very active.* She was great for him, though, because everything was very on schedule and routine. She always had lunch at the same time, nap time, craft time, and playtime. Cooper did well if he had the same routine, and he learned to adapt to the familiar activities.

Later, when Lisa went back to work outside the home as a preschool teacher, Cooper was one of her students. I loved this arrangement because he already knew her, and she was great at working with kids. When we had his three-year-old preschool review, she told me about his behaviors of fidgeting, interrupting, and bothering others, as well as his inability to sit and focus. He was young and my first child, so I asked her, "Is this normal?"

Her answer would ring in my ears for years to come. She said, "No, Not really."

My thoughts raced. "What do you mean?"

Lisa replied, "He is more fidgety and distracted than the other kids. He can't sit still, and he demands a great deal of attention."

Though the preschool was good for Cooper, we had to find additional childcare to have care for him for all the hours that we worked. We found a new and very experienced provider, Daphne, who checked all the boxes. She had sixteen years of experience, and she cared for many children who were Cooper's age. There was even one little girl whom he had been with in his previous daycare at Lisa's house and was also in her preschool with him. I felt so blessed to find him another sitter in town. God had blessed us because good sitters were hard to come by, and sometimes there was a waiting list. This sitter was also close to my work, and I could pick him up on the way home.

Cooper was also progressing well physically on the growth charts. He was in the ninety-ninth percentile for his height and weight. He was going to be a big boy just like his dad, who was six foot, five inches tall.

After Cooper had been at this new daycare for more than a year, I pulled up to pick him up after work one day, not knowing the trajectory of my life was about to change. Daphne told me that she needed to talk to me about him.

Okay, *What is up?* I thought. *Is it his turn to bring treats?* Instead, she told me she could not keep Cooper anymore. I was shocked. I asked her why. She then told me that he took too much attention, and he bothered the other kids. It took too much extra

79

time to watch him, she continued. Caring for him took her away from the other kids.

I thought, *What, my child is too much? You have had how many children go through here, and all of a sudden, you can't keep my child anymore?* I was surprised, and I tried to contain myself. I told her I would talk to my husband, but we needed some time. I didn't really understand what had just happened. I was immediately in a position to find another new place for him, and I really needed to look at his needs more closely. I quickly called Doug, who was still at work. He wasn't sure what to think.

During the next few weeks, I found someone who could keep Cooper temporarily but not long-term because she was close to her daycare limit with number of kids. I agreed that it would be temporary, so my husband and I took a close look at our lives and how we might handle our upcoming situation. Doug and I talked about what to do, and we decided that I needed to have a different schedule.

I had been at my job almost ten years, and I thought I would be there forever. I loved my job and the people I worked with, but I loved my child more. He had to come first.

We knew Cooper would not be ready for kindergarten because of his immaturity and his attention span. Our local school, however, had just begun offering a transitional kindergarten, which was to help five-year-olds not quite ready for kindergarten learn about the way the school functioned. This setup seemed perfect for him because he could stay at his temporary daycare until he was ready for school.

We decided that I would apply for a job in our school district as the technology coordinator. I got the job. It was bittersweet. I was sad to leave my old job, as I mentioned, but I understood bigger things were at play with my son.

My new school schedule was somewhat flexible with summers off, which gave me more time to watch him during that part of the year. I could also do some of my work at night at school while Doug was home to watch Cooper. I don't know if it was my bipolar or just an odd schedule, but I had always felt my brain worked well in the middle of the night when no one was around. It was also nice for me to be working more with computers than I had been previously doing. I think God knows that I have challenges with my emotions, but as I have shared previously, I appreciated that computers never talk back! I always got along with them no matter what mood I was in; they didn't care if I laughed or cried while I worked on them.

Cooper was full of energy, always running and climbing. When his grandparents were around him, they anxiously watched for him to tumble. I already knew he might fall, so I had grown to expect it, although that didn't make dealing with his energy easy in any way! He had a history of going so fast that it got him into trouble. One time, he raced toward the road as I screamed for him to stop. Another time, I got a call from the daycare that he ran into a flowerpot and needed stitches. Then, he ran headfirst into my grandma's coffee table and needed stitches again. Because of an accident during which he fell off the monkey bars at the park and broke his arm, Cooper started transitional kindergarten with a cast on his arm. He was an adorable boy with way too much energy. But he was a boy, and they are made of "snakes and snails and puppy dog tails."

He had extra tactile sensitivities with his clothes. He didn't like tags in his shirts, and certain socks weren't comfortable if they had a seam that bothered him. He could not get past these things. After some counseling and psychological testing during that transitional kindergarten year, we learned that he had ADHD and (Obsessive Compulsive Disorder) OCD. These disorders were noticed as he progressed through kindergarten and beyond in school because his teachers continued to see that he could not sit still and fidgeted.

Even though he came up with the right answers for questions, he couldn't do it as quickly as the other students, especially in math. Working at his own pace was something we had to work with the teachers on because they were so insistent that things follow a normal time frame. By the time Cooper began third grade, he was recommended for the resource room and accommodations so he could do his work at his own pace and in a quiet setting. He was able to do much better and had an Individual Education Plan (IEP). This development helped greatly with his work. He was given leeway to get it done, but he started having homework, which meant hours at home doing homework with him. It was grueling, but we were devoted to his well-being. However, this routine began to take a toll on our marriage. Working with him took so much effort that Doug and I were exhausted when he went to bed, and we had little time for each other.

I mentioned that I got into a habit of working in the middle of the night to stay on top of things. I eventually transitioned to part-time in the job I had at the school with someone else leading the department instead of me doing it. I wanted to be with Cooper more. With this role, I was able to be with Cooper after school. I still went to school at night to check things on the computer network. The police at first stopped to see what was going on that late at night or early in the morning, but after a while, they knew my car and just let me be.

Doug was growing weary of my alarm going off in the middle of the night and the way this schedule was affecting my bipolar illness at times because of my lack of sleep. But this type of late-night activity is not uncommon in those with bipolar. I tried to reason with my husband that I had to operate this way for my son. I pushed myself harder to get things done than anyone else did.

I also worried that I had genetically passed down something to Cooper. I had been different and labeled, and I hated that my son was now being labeled different too. *Had I caused this?* I had so much guilt and misunderstanding about what was going on. *Would he be bipolar too?* I feared this outcome for him. But I trusted God to lead us whatever happened next.

When he was in third grade and on an IEP that I mentioned earlier, Cooper was referred to a different doctor and retested. That doctor gave him a diagnosis of borderline Asperger's, a form of autism in which the person is mainly high functioning, but social and developmental challenges still occur.[8] People with Asperger's may also shows signs of ADHD and OCD, which

Cooper did. His behaviors made more sense with the added diagnosis of Asperger's. Learning about his new diagnosis and how the different conditions played off of each other helped us understand why he had problems with fitting in with the other kids, making friends, and doing work fast.

He was put on medication, but some of the medication made the OCD worse. It was a struggle to get the correct medication for him, and it was difficult to get him the needed support at school and at home, but we worked hard at it. He was also put on a 504 plan, which is part of the Americans with Disabilities Act.[9] This program, as an addition to his IEP, allowed him to have more accommodations to help his learning process. He was given a quiet room with a special instructor to take tests where there were no distractions. He also was allowed to do every other problem in math since he was accurate but slower to come up with the answers. If he needed a quiet space, he could leave the room to go the resource room, which only had a few people at a time in it.

Much more was in store for us as we continued to parent Cooper and deal with his diagnoses, but the biggest part for us, just like with my bipolar illness, was acceptance and moving forward in a positive way.

These disabilities were real, but we needed to make sure we didn't let them define us. So Doug and I constantly told ourselves, "Cooper is Cooper, and we need to accept and adjust to his needs." This statement was easy to say, but it wasn't easy to do. We often wondered, *What would the next several years hold for us?* For the sake of all of us, we would need to learn to take everything one day at a time. We recommitted to continuing the specific routines and time spent helping him with school work. Though we had taken the first step of acceptance, we would need endurance to run this race with Cooper.

Chapter Ten

Believing in Unexpected Blessings

Though helping Cooper took a toll on Doug and me during the week, when we were in church, our relationship grew as we looked to God for help and guidance. I loved how Doug would hold my hand during prayer. Once we left church and got busy with our everyday life, however, we both returned to our stubbornness.

As I've mentioned, I didn't get married until I was thirty-two. I had grown accustomed to getting my way because I was the only one who got a vote. Doug had been married previously and divorced before we met. He, too, was settled into his ways of doing things. Sometimes, it seemed like when I said black, he said white, and vice versa. We are both oldest children too, which only reinforced our propensity to each be in charge.

I believed it was wise to ask God about every decision, and I would even say, "We should pray about this before we make a decision." We both would even agree by saying, "Yes, we should."

So many times, however, I did not listen to my own thoughts or words. Looking back, I can see that we were both immature in our faith. We had always called ourselves Christians, but God really wasn't incorporated into our day-to-day life. Our daily work schedules would get busy, and so, like many new couples, our praying and worship were done mainly on Sundays. I loved being in church together and worshiping, so I'm not sure why I didn't do more to involve God into our everyday life.

Although we both liked being right, neither one of us wanted to rock the boat and cause disagreements. Our schedules and avoidance, therefore, led to miscommunication. I truly believe God put us together to refine us and help us grow. As the potter, our marriage was His way of taking our bumps and flaws and smoothing them out for our own good and growth. We were forced to seek God's help and realignment to deal with Cooper's challenges.

As I mentioned earlier, when Cooper was old enough to attend school all day, I changed my schedule to part-time at the school. Doing so helped me drop him off in the mornings and pick him up after school. This schedule was a welcome change for Doug, too, because I tended to be a workaholic, and part-time forced me to regain some balance in my life. Staying home in the afternoons helped me be a housewife in the afternoon before I picked up Cooper from school. I had time to take care of the home, where I really felt in my element. I enjoyed cooking, and Doug was happy to have meals ready when he got home. I flourished as a wife and mother. I decided it was my true calling.

By the time Cooper was about five, the maternal instinct that I had fostered by raising him contributed to my longing for another child. I was approaching forty, and I knew my biological clock was ticking. My hormones and emotions were all over the place. I would cry and get upset, and I became convinced my happiness was dependent on another child. My body and my mind would not let go of the pangs of my heart.

As soon as I talked to Doug about another child, I realized there was a significant problem. Earlier in our marriage, after we had Cooper, Doug and I experienced a serious miscommunication. He had a vasectomy because he thought we both wanted that done. But as my heart yearned for another child, I was questioning that decision, wondering why I hadn't thought more about it at the time…

"I don't even remember you asking or talking about this." I said.

Doug with a sheepish look on his face, "I thought we talked about it. I know you remember me sitting in the recliner with ice."

"Yes, I guess I didn't register what it meant at the time."

He was even more frustrated that he couldn't fix it. He replied, "I'm really sorry, but I can't do anything about it now."

"I know, I said, and I think that maybe I was so busy raising Cooper in his early stages that perhaps I hadn't even remembered that we discussed it earlier."

Since my previously buried dream of a larger family seemed impossible with this realization, I cried as I begged for God to intervene.

I couldn't believe I didn't remember discussing it. Maybe we talked briefly. Regardless, five years earlier, the deed had been done. What can we do now God? I did not feel like I was given an emphatic no to my plea. Was there some hope?

I knew I had dreamed and prayed about a baby girl; that was all I could think about. I was so upset, and Doug knew my feelings were not going to change. He wasn't happy about this development, but he knew I wouldn't relent. My hormones were still raging, too. All I kept thinking about was, *What were we going to do to fix this?*

We looked online, and we decided he should have a vasectomy reversal. We made an appointment to go to a specialist in Chicago. Our appointment was set, and we would embark on the beginning of a journey only God could have orchestrated. The trip took ten hours, which gave us plenty of time to talk about getting ready for the next step. We got there the night before the procedure and spent the night in a hotel, but it was hard to sleep.

The next morning at the appointment, the waiting room was filled with people with scheduled same-day surgeries. *Was there someone else here who was doing what we were doing?* Doug was very quiet before the procedure and probably wondered what landed him in this precarious situation. The surgery was a little over an hour, and then he came out in pain but ready to go home. I graciously walked hand in hand with him to the van. I was the driver now. I drove him back on that ten-hour journey from Chicago to Iowa as he recovered with ice, lying on a mattress in the back of our van.

"Watch out for bumps," he would say.

He must love me to do what he just did, I thought. A vasectomy was not fun the first time, but it takes longer to repair and recover from the reversal. I had asked a lot of him, but he knew it had to be done. I had a dream of a little girl. She would not leave my mind. I was happy that we had taken a step toward that dream, but I did feel bad about the pain Doug was going through at that moment.

As the months went on, he was tested to see if the reversal had worked, and we were told that it did. We began trying to make that baby I knew was in our future. But I was almost forty, and perimenopause and my biological clock weren't cooperating.

There were countless pregnancy tests, and all were negative. There were, of course, many tears on my part. Doug was disappointed too because he had now decided another child was a good idea. He, however, was growing weary of the process. You wouldn't think a man could get tired of sex, but when it is a mission, it isn't as much fun. He could also see my face when a negative test came back when I had been sure that I was pregnant. It was like a balloon being popped every time.

After one of those popped balloons when I was feeling discouraged, somehow, I thought back to when we were first married. Doug said back then that he didn't think he wanted to have any kids, but I had reassured him that he would be a good dad. I brushed it off, thinking, *Oh, everyone wants kids; he just doesn't know it yet.* He and I had sometimes put words into each other's mouths, but we made assumptions in our thoughts more often.

Eventually, however, we usually ended up, after we expressed our thoughts and discussed the matter, God willing, with better results. This time, as we sought to expand our family, would be no different. I was looking at the way Doug reacted to Cooper; he couldn't have been more thrilled. He was almost giddy. Doug could look back to when Cooper was born and be reassured of his instant fatherly love. He knew us having him was meant to be —just like I did. And similarly, Doug had believed we were meant to grow our family.

One day several months after his reversal and no luck conceiving, Doug came up with the idea that we should talk to Joe and Kate, our friends who had adopted through Holt International. I was first surprised that he suggested it. But then I was also so happy that I felt like my spirit was soaring. Doug and I thought about our friends' daughter from South Korea, who was three years old, beautiful, and such a blessing in their life.

When we approached them, I shared my apprehension: "I'm nervous about adopting, but we want to go international like you two did. Otherwise, I would have a fear of my daughter being taken back by the mother. I know I am being paranoid, but I also know I will bond with her right away. I've heard too many stories of heartbreak with domestic adoption."

"I understand," Joe replied. "Also, tell the agency that you want a healthy baby if you do not wish to have a child with special needs. They will try to match your request."

The adoption was going to be a financial stretch for us, and we had to borrow money. The $20,000 price tag didn't deter us. There was no turning back; we would start the adoption process. We contacted the same adoption agency our friends used and began the paperwork. And my goodness, there was a lot of paperwork, hoops to jump through, home studies, and classes to attend.

Months went by as we waited for the word from Holt that there was a baby for us. I tried to put the wait and my desire out of my mind, but I couldn't. I prayed to God, writing out prayers asking for my future daughter. *God, I know you are probably getting tired of hearing from me.*

The adoption process was worse than being pregnant as far as the waiting and anticipation went. At least when giving birth, you know the amount of time you must wait and can feel your baby moving inside of you. I must admit, I got a little discouraged at various times. I started buying baby girl clothes and things for my sweet daughter to prepare for her arrival once we were approved by the adoption agency. I was excited and nervous all at the same time. I was trusting Him with the hope that He was bringing me as I continued to raise my son and pray for my daughter-to-be.

We even got Cooper's old crib back out and put it in our room. I knew I wanted her close to me. We knew it would be a girl because the people we talked to said you would get what you requested. We asked for a healthy baby girl from South Korea. We decided not to ask for special needs, even though we have a heart for that.

I will always remember the day my family was in church, and I prayed for my baby girl. It was like I opened my eyes, and I could see a vision of Jesus walking down the center aisle of the church towards me, carrying a baby. My heart leapt with excitement. There had been times I thought I saw bright angel wings through the church-stained glass windows, but this vision was different—it was so real. Though I didn't try, it seemed like I could reach out and touch the wings.

After having that realistic vision of an angel, God finally brought my heart peace as He leveled my mind by increasing my faith and revealing His love. I couldn't believe that He loved me enough to show me something so special. From that moment on, I knew everything would work out just the way it was supposed to, and I was thrilled. I thanked God for His amazing blessing. I was truly going to bring my baby girl home. I had cried and talked to God, longing for my vision to come to pass soon. I no longer had any doubt. I told Doug about this vision, and we were both ecstatic! We celebrated and continued to prepare for her arrival. We had no idea when it would be, but we knew God had our daughter in His hands, and soon, she would be in ours.

The total process of adoption took thirteen months, which doesn't seem like that long, but a yearning heart tells the mind a different story.

Around Thanksgiving 2002, we finally got the call that changed our life forever. I couldn't contain my excitement as I held my hand over the phone and shared the news with Doug.

"Our new daughter was born in South Korea! Praise God!" We hugged each other in anticipation of the day we would meet her.

Holt also sent us a beautiful picture of our three-day-old baby. I couldn't stop looking at her picture, and I showed everyone whether they wanted to see it or not. She looked very healthy, and she had lots of black hair!

She would have to be in foster care for a few months before coming to us because they needed to do the well-baby checks, and there was more paperwork and classes to do.

Earlier in the process, we had completed all our home studies, during which I had relayed to the social worker that I had a diagnosis of bipolar, but I also relayed that I was managing it well. It had made me a little nervous to disclose that information, but I had wanted to be totally honest. I believe that they appreciated that.

After we were matched, we continued the adoption process by taking classes to teach us about our baby and her culture. In these meetings, we were also given the opportunity to take time to be with others who were adopting. We got to talk with those families about the upcoming changes we would soon encounter. Having that support to know we weren't alone in what we were experiencing was essential. The agency also offered services and connections as we raised our new child along with heritage trips for families to visit her country of origin when she was older. This information was all part of the training, which would help us navigate raising a child from another country so we could share their culture as part of their upbringing.

That time in our lives was exciting. Our son, Cooper, was about seven at the time. We told him he was getting a sister, and he too was excited about her arrival. I talked to him about how to hold and play with his sister.

On April 14th, 2003, the agency called and said, "You and your husband can go to the airport in Omaha on April 22nd at 5:30

p.m. and pick up your new daughter. She will be brought by an escort from the adoption agency."

Shortly after that phone call, we received her medical and developmental updates. We read them again and again. We still couldn't believe that we were holding her flight itinerary in our hands! I said to Doug, "In one week, she'll be coming home! Praise God!"

We couldn't help but share the good news of her arrival with our friends, family, and the church. Everyone who knew us was happy for us as we finished our baby preparations.

April 22nd came, and we drove two and a half hours to the Omaha airport as a family of three. We would be returning as a family of four. It was a beautiful sunny day—as if God had put an exclamation point on it. This agency had given us a choice: go to Korea to pick her up or have an agency escort to fly her to America. We chose the latter because we didn't want to leave our son, who was a handful, unpredictable, and difficult at times.

The three of us waited in the Omaha airport with another couple who had a baby boy coming on the same plane. Cooper played with the couple's older boy, who was also waiting to be a big brother. They had many family members with them and a big bunch of balloons. Doug and I, however, were glad to have just the three of us there to meet our new family member. We didn't want to overwhelm our weary traveler when she got off the plane.

The wait seemed like forever, but it was only an hour or so, and we realized people were getting off the plane. Our eyes scanned every person as they walked toward us, anxiously awaiting our sweet baby girl. Then, in the back, we saw two Korean women with babies starting to walk toward us. *Which baby was ours?*

Our daughter's escort was the younger of the two, and she was headed right towards us. I was so thankful for her, and I wondered if it had been hard for her to care for a baby on that fourteen-hour flight to America.

My heart nearly leapt out of my chest as this young woman placed our long-awaited daughter in my loving arms. I had been given a baby sling to hold her close and calm her. Placing her in it and having it around me was like having a warm hug from God Himself. I couldn't stop smiling. Doug had tears in his eyes, too. I thanked the escort; we told her this meant the world to us. She gave us a baby album and an authentic Korean costume that came from the foster parents who had watched over our baby in South Korea.

Our baby had arrived safely from her long journey, and from that point on, she would be with us. Suddenly, a culmination of emotions from the last few years streamed down my face. They were happy tears. We had a beautiful, healthy baby. She was five months old, and we decided to call her Olivia. Her middle name is Grace because God's Grace brought her to us. Her Korean name is Hye-Rin Park.

I couldn't stop looking at Olivia. I loved seeing all the black hair I had looked at so many times in her newborn picture in person. She looked like a Korean Gerber baby. She had multiple layers of clothes and was bundled up, probably to keep her calm on her long flight to America. We all took our turns holding our sweet baby.

On that day, there was nothing but love all around. The trouble that Doug and I had sometimes in communication wasn't present on that precious Tuesday afternoon, which we now refer to as Olivia's Gotcha day. What a perfect sunny April day in 2003.

Cooper was thrilled to have a little sister. Doug was protective of us all, especially his daughter, as we got ready to go home. I then did what moms do and went to the bathroom to change sweet Olivia's diaper from the long trip. I unpacked the bundles she was in to get to her sweet body and made sure she was dry and happy. We gathered her things, and just like that, we were ready to head home.

The feeling was unreal. I felt excitement for sure, but also, we had a feeling of slight uncertainty. *Can we just leave the airport with our baby and go home?*

We confirmed with our adoption host that we could take Olivia home, and we said our goodbyes to her and the other family that was there as we exchanged hugs and wished everyone well.

Olivia cried a little on the way home, so I sat in the back seat to be near her to comfort her. She especially got upset when a big semi-truck went by and made a loud noise. *She must have had enough noise on the plane and needed a quiet place to rest*, I thought.

Our journey to Olivia taught us so much about how God works all things together beautifully. We knew the journey of adoption had always been in His hands. Taking her home was the culmination of months of waiting and praying, coming to realization, and it was truly perfect. In the car ride home, we felt that all was right with the world as we felt the heartfelt joy oozing out of us. Everyone was thanking God for our sweet Olivia as we drove.

When we got home, our friends had put a "Welcome Home Olivia" sign on our garage. It was wonderful to walk into the house with her. We were instructed to cocoon her, which meant we would just have the three of us around her for the first week or so to let her settle in. Even though it was hard to keep people away, that time alone with her was the most precious time for our family. Olivia Grace Brunsting was part of our family forever. Thank You, God, for your rich blessings! She is the daughter that was born and placed in our hearts and minds. What I had previously thought were detours and delays was actually divine direction and destiny—I can't imagine it any other way!

C hapter E leven

BEING REMINDED OF GRANDMA'S LOVE

A dopting Olivia was one of the happiest times of my life, but the road to bringing her home in 2003 also was marked by the difficulty of my grandma's passing in 2002. Just after Grandma's memorial, I was given one tangible item that gave me more comfort than any other as I was preparing to be a mother to my baby girl: a handwritten letter. I would often carefully retrieve the letter from its place of safekeeping during that preparatory time and beyond.

As I write this book decades later, the letter is torn and faded; the paper is yellowed. Reading it was so healing because it was one item God used to get me past the insecure feelings of still being a little girl inside. Growing up with Dad's anger and Mom's unhappiness, I often was unsure of where I belonged and questioned their love. But, as I have mentioned, I always felt safe and loved at Grandma's. Her letter helped me remember her love. Reading it brought back my fond memories of being a child.

Grandma's example of loving me unconditionally showed me how I wanted to raise my own children. My daughter was not only my new sweet baby, but she was God's, and I wanted to respect the gift He had given us through adoption. This tangible reminder and Grandma's steadfast love helped pave my way on the journey God had entrusted me to.

My grandma wrote:

Teresa Lynn Newman. My first Grandbaby was born on December 19, 1961. What a Joy to behold. So sweet, so cute. A baby girl, with not much hair, not even a curl. Just the cutest baby I ever saw. Now doesn't that sound like I'm a grandma? I called all my relatives and wrote to all my friends. Blue eyes, brown hair, not much, just perfect, you know. She looks like her dad, and some like her mother. Oh, so loved, there can't be another. Her name is Teresa Lynn. She's stolen our hearts, and I'm sure she even knows her grandmother. Grandpa, Uncle, and Aunt all gaze at her. Well, she is just great, we're telling you.

The letter affirmed what I felt when I was with Grandma—that I was a "normal" little girl. My grandma had shown me care in a gentle way since the day I was born, and I loved her so much! There may have been times when I did something naughty that she didn't like my behavior and then she showed some disappointment. She never, however, denied me love.

Grandma didn't show anger like my parents did. Mom and Dad would fly off the handle. Since much of their discipline was with anger, I thought that I needed to protect myself. I didn't learn from this type of discipline. Grandma, however, showed firm but calm discipline that I craved. I suppose I felt love from her because I could be myself. I felt like my grandma always put me first.

As I have shared, I loved her cooking. In addition to her famous mashed potatoes, she made great pot roast and heavenly seasoned green beans. Nor will I ever forget the taste of her delicious potato soup. Her amazing homemade food was one way she showed her devotion to her family.

She also let me have adventures by encouraging me to play freely. It was wonderful and so much fun to run around the farm —and to use my imagination to create make-believe stories. I remember being a young child, around seven and being out in the yard after a spring rain. My aunt and uncle would shake the trees over me. We would pretend we were making it rain by shaking the branches and standing under them while getting drenched.

We pretended to cook by making mud pies and adding extra garden ingredients like spoiled vegetables that Grandma gave us. I was never bored because nature was all around me. We always had a blast through our years as kids at Grandma's. In the winter, we would sled down a big hill in the pasture. In the summer, I would chase butterflies and play with the cats and dogs. I loved to go in the hayloft and find baby kittens who hadn't even opened their eyes. Another favorite of ours was when we would go to the watermelon patch and take our middle finger and thumb and thump to check to see if the watermelons were ripe. When they were ripe, we had a watermelon feast.

Whether I was running around, making mud pies, or checking out the garden, I often came in dirty. Grandma didn't yell at me, but she was firm and fair. She would say, "March to the bathroom and get yourself cleaned up." After I did as she said, she would give me a snack I loved—either Rice Krispies bars, fresh cut-up apples, or homemade cookies. Her love made behaving a desire, not a task.

I can't think of anything I didn't like at Grandma's house, nor anytime I didn't enjoy being there. Not only did I enjoy naps on her bed, but the big, puffy blankets felt like a hug at night when I would spend the night. Just like during my naps, I would pull the covers up high on my neck. I could hear Grandma and Grandpa talking in the next room about chores to do on the farm, the weather, and what other relatives were doing. I felt so safe and warm as I drifted off to sleep; hearing my grandparents' voices quieted the worrying part of me.

Grandma's countenance had comforted me just as much as her voice did. Her radiant soul was apparent in the pictures that were around her house and through her life. She was as beautiful on the outside as she was on the inside. Her skin was vibrant, too. As I was growing up, I liked touching her face, which was made smooth by her nightly wash with Noxzema. I laugh today at how wonderful her skin was then, and she did so little to keep it that way. Fresh air and sunshine also gave her a healthy tan.

Despite Grandma's outer and inner beauty, I knew that she had withstood many hardships in life, including the most difficult—the loss of children. Grandma had one daughter who died one day after birth. As a child, Grandma also witnessed the death of an eight-year-old sister to pneumonia. She also had become a widow twice.

She had to deal with her own physical ailments, including asthma and allergies. But she never really complained, and she always showed the love she had for Jesus, her family, and me. It was easy to see her love, especially through her eyes. People say the eyes are the windows to the soul, and her eyes allowed her beautiful soul and spirit to shine bright.

Her spirit was strong until she took her last breath and went to her heavenly home to be with Jesus. I will never forget that day. Mom had called to tell me Grandma was in the hospital, dying. I immediately drove five hours to see her. The time driving was like silent torture. I couldn't get there any faster, and I cried and prayed to see my grandma again. I loved her so.

When I got to the waiting room, I heard from my aunt and uncle, "She waited for you to get here, Teresa. She is hanging on for you."

I quickly made my way to her room shaking all over.

As I walked into her hospital room and saw her lying on the bed, my heart sank. I began to cry by her bedside.

My dad, who was already in the room with her, kept saying to her, "God and Jesus...God and Jesus. It's okay for you to rest in them."

I looked at her tired eyes. I held Grandma's hand, and with other family in the room, Grandma's breathing started to slow. Then it was time; she breathed her last breath. I was so glad to make it to her side in time to say goodbye. Those moments were precious beyond words.

From her letter, I knew she remembered my first days, and I remember what an impact she had on me from my earliest memories until her last breath. She was, is—and will always be—in my heart. After she died, I also received pictures of her that I hadn't seen before. I have always loved—and still love—to look at pictures of her. Her pictures, along with the letter, help keep her spirit alive to me.

When I am discouraged, I remember her love. It was like Jesus' and God's love, which is unconditional. I think she instilled in me a resilience that I always want to live with and carry as I move forward. Thinking about her, reading her letter, and snuggling up in Grandma's homemade quilt gives me hope. Even though sometimes I have to consciously fight to keep that hope alive, between her spirit and the Holy Spirit, they both help keep hope alive deep in my spirit.

Even at times when I saw no hope in my life when I was going through struggles, I knew that she wanted the best for me. It is hard to think of how loved you are sometimes when you are in the pit, but I tell you for sure that what I learned from Grandma is true: We all are loved by God. God knew us before we were born when we were in our mother's womb. He delights in us when we draw near to Him and wants us to know that there is a plan for us, no matter how we try to mess it up. The more I look back at where God was in my life, the more I am amazed. He has always been—and is still—always there.

As I mentioned earlier in the book, I first met God in my grandma's country church. There, I learned a song I still love to sing:

Jesus loves me. This I know, for the Bible tells me so.
Little ones to Him belong; they are weak, but He is strong.

I never doubted the words in that song as a child because when I asked Grandma about it, she told me it was true. She also lived out His love as she interacted with me. The old hymns that we sang in Grandma's church have always remained in my heart as well. We sang "Amazing Grace" at her funeral. I am reminded of her anytime I hear it.

Grandma's example of resilience would help as I walked through my own fires with His help. I remembered her church and the stories I learned there. I knew as I faced each new struggle in life that I could get through anything just like the Bible story I first learned in her church about Shadrach, Meshach, and Abednego, who walked through the fiery furnace with Jesus. I knew I would walk through whatever came my way with Jesus, too—even the struggles of dealing with bipolar. Grandma's deep faith was deep inside of me. After her death, I hoped to reaffirm what I knew all along in my heart—no matter what, I wanted to walk with Jesus just as she did. She was a great role model in life and to this day, I continue to do my best to become more like her.

I also learned in therapy, years after her death that times of reflection on good times and bad brought out the lessons learned, which in turn, paved a way to begin to heal and function better.

I also remember being introduced to the concept of finding a healthy coping mechanism at some point in counseling. A coping mechanism resets the mind just like a computer restart helps a computer properly function. Reading my grandma's letter that she wrote to me as a baby became one of those coping mechanism for me. Her words help me find "normal" Teresa again. They help level my mind by bringing peace because they remind me of the truth that I am enough simply because I am unconditionally loved as a child of God.

Chapter Twelve

LEVELING MY MOODS

Whenever I struggled with my moods and emotions, I would need to level them so they would not be too high or too low. Although everyone is different, for me, this process of balancing my moods was needed about once a month, or more frequently, depending on my stress level.

I would either be manic with heightened emotions, or I would find myself very down. After this cycle happened a few times, Doug could tell when it was happening. When I was on the depressive side, one of my coping mechanisms would be to snuggle with Grandma's quilt, read her letter, and watch my favorite movie, *It's a Wonderful Life*, starring Jimmy Stewart—the black and white version.[10] It has been my favorite for many decades. I first got attached to this movie as a young adult after my suicide attempt in my twenties. I had seen it before with my parents, but after that incident, it began to hit home.

In the very beginning of the movie, two angels are talking in Heaven, to a third angel. One of those angels, Clarence, is told he would get his wings, which, according to the movie, is akin to passing angel training, if he helped a man named George Bailey. ZuZu, George's young daughter was praying for her dad and told God, "Something's the matter with Daddy...please bring Daddy home."

Even George himself sought God when he said, "Dear Father in heaven, I'm not a praying man, but if you're up there and you can hear me, show me the way...show me the way."

Joseph, one of the angels, commented to Clarence, "A lot of people are praying for a man named George Bailey."

Clarence asked, "Is he sick?"

Joseph responded, "No, worse. He's discouraged, and he is thinking about throwing away God's greatest gift."

Clarence replied, "Oh dear, dear, his life..."

Joseph then took Clarence back through George's life so he could get to know him from the time he was a boy until his crucial day, the day before Christmas when he found out their company was on the verge of losing all their money.

George was told by the meanest and richest man in town, Mr. Potter, when he tried to use a life insurance policy as collateral to get a loan, that he was worth more dead than alive.

George, at his lowest point, even said to Clarence, "Maybe it would have been better if I were never born."

Clarence then takes George on a journey to show what his life had truly meant to others, as if he had never been born. George finally saw how valuable he was to not only his family, but to the community and to God. He then said, "Please God, let me live again."

As I watch the movie, I relate to George Bailey, who also contemplated ending it all during one of his times of trouble. I resonate with his sadness and feel his pain, but I am also reminded of my own worth as George was shown his worth as the movie progressed. His friends came through for him, and Clarence won his wings. In the book he gave to George, he wrote, "No man is a failure who has friends."

I have watched this movie hundreds of times during every season of the year. It is not just a Christmas movie to me. It resets my thinking. When I am discouraged, I need that kind of encouragement to bring me back up to a balanced level.

I especially love the part where Clarence, the angel, summarizes the journey of what he has just shown George about his value. "You see, George, you've really had a wonderful life. Don't you see what a mistake it would be to throw it all away?"

Clarence continues, "Strange, isn't it? Each man's life touches so many other lives. When he isn't around, he leaves an awful hole, doesn't he?"

Those words make me cry every time I watch it. The entire movie causes an emotional release, which helps me get out of being on the lower part of the bipolar cycle.

Whenever I watch the movie, I pray and ask for the Father, Son, and Holy Spirit to come in the form of First aid from the Holy Spirit, who dwells inside me. I am able then to calm myself and rest in God's promise that He will never leave nor forsake me.

However I get back to a normal level by resetting my emotions, I remind myself that I am loved and a part of something bigger. For as long as I can remember, I have longed to find my purpose. Although the correlation isn't direct, somehow, the movie and Grandma's letter, help me see myself as a beloved child of God. I have purpose, then, to simply be His child. I know I am valuable to family and friends, just as George was loved by those close to Him. I also believe, deep down, that because God began a work in me, He will finish it in His time. Whenever I need to be more tangibly reminded of my purpose, I use one of these coping mechanisms that I've come to treasure.

If I asked George Bailey today to give me advice about dealing with my mental illness, he would probably say something like:

> I understand what it feels like to think the world would be better off without you. I've stood on a bridge, feeling like a failure, thinking I didn't matter. But an angel showed me that I was wrong. You, like me, would be surprised how many lives you've touched just by being alive. Each of us don't always see the difference we make. But we do make a difference.
>
> Life can be messy, hard, and sometimes downright unfair. But it's also full of victories, friends, second chances, and love that shows up when you least expect it.
>
> Don't give up. Don't give in. Your friends and family need you more than you know. Someday, you'll look back and see that even the hardest days were part of something beautiful.

I am so grateful that God gave me amazing gifts to help me cope. The letter, quilt, and movie continue to comfort me. The first two are ways to remember Grandma and all those who made an impact on my life. The movie also reminds me that I am valuable, too. I make a difference just by being here—just like my friends and family tell me I do.

112

My friend, you matter too. If you sometimes doubt that, maybe watch It's a Wonderful Life, *find a treasured keepsake, or ask God to show you His love for you in a special way that is unique to you.*

C hapter T hirteen

DISRUPTING THE JOURNEY

There was a season in our life that felt almost normal with everyday busyness, but beneath the surface, it was quietly unraveling. The kids were growing, my marriage seemed stable, but looking back now as I write, I can see where the cracks began in my relationship with Doug. I can remember having an inkling that something was wrong, but nothing to base it on so I began to push those feelings aside with distractions—kids, friends, and looking for a bigger home for our family.

Cooper was nine, and Olivia was two. I had hopes for years of living in one particular beautiful home—my old boss's home—that I had first seen when I first came to Orange City with my mom nearly eighteen years earlier. I had previously told him that if he ever sold it to let me know. So, that year, when my boss put his house up for sale, he kept his word and told me. Doug knew I had always loved it, and he liked it too, so we decided to purchase it. Buying the home was a stretch for us financially which added to our financial burden, but fulfilling this dream was important to us. My dream of living in this Spanish stucco house was coming to fruition!

We made the arrangements and prepared to move. Packing as we were managing Cooper's needs and a toddler was no small task, but I was excited about having my dream of living in that house fulfilled. We made some updates we wanted to the home and moved in.

At that point, Doug and I had been married for close to twelve years. Like any couple, we both had made some mistakes and had our share of challenges. I was, from time to time, still struggling with my bipolar and all that goes with it, but I thought we were happy. I trusted that we were. I felt "normal"—or at least I thought things were normal—until I later learned they weren't...

In actuality, the issues started bubbling silently the year prior to us moving. Doug turned forty in 2004, and I had begun planning to have a fortieth birthday party for him several weeks before that February to celebrate his milestone. I invited our friends and people from his work. We decided to get a sitter for the event. I got to the party early to make sure the food and drinks were all ready. I had been at the venue that afternoon to decorate with pictures of Doug all through his life for people to look at. It was fun. I enjoyed party planning.

People started arriving, and I greeted them.

"There are snacks and drinks in the lounge. Thanks for coming. Doug will be happy to see you all."

"Where is the old guy?" a friend responded jokingly.

I pointed to the lounge.

I was still visiting with a few people and enjoying myself when I glanced across the room to see one of Doug's female coworkers, Blair, give him a big hug that lasted a little too long. She then kissed him on the cheek. Her husband was there too. I

116

wondered if her husband had seen the affection his wife and Doug had for one another. What I saw gave me a strange, uncomfortable feeling. I didn't like it, but I decided I was making too much of it. When we got home that night, I said, "What is up with you and Blair? I don't trust her as far as I could throw her." *I sounded like Toni,* I thought.

He said, "I don't want to talk about it. I'm going to bed."

"You're welcome for the birthday party by the way," I said smugly. "I still don't trust her. If you said you want to mess around, I know she would say yes. She is that kind of girl. I trust you, but I don't trust her."

"I'm done talking about this," he said as he left the room.

I began to cry.

This incident was not the first time I felt uncomfortable with this woman around. Doug was her boss, and many times, they were out at night with vendors, and there was drinking involved. I didn't understand why he always had to go out at night to socialize.

In the past, when I went out late to do work, I had the actual purpose of completing a task, and I thought his evening events were frivolous and unnecessary. I especially didn't feel good about her being there nor did I comprehend why she had to be involved. I would voice my problem with this situation, but it fell on deaf ears. I tried to tell him that work should be done during work hours, unless it was an emergency. I definitely didn't think it was healthy for him to go out for work events at night all the time. I told him I understood engaging in company business on the golf course, but that I didn't understand why Blair always had to be there. I was getting worn out trying to make my point. I would bring it up now and then, but for the most part, I tried to move on because my concerns only caused arguments.

I loved having a husband and two wonderful children. My plate was full, and I trusted everything would be okay.

I was still struggling with my moods, though, at times. My moods for the most part had stabilized for me over the years with a consistent relationship, medication, healthy habits, and therapy. But occasionally the illness would rear its ugly head. It was especially hard to control with the fact that Doug and I were arguing more.

Many times I would get so upset that I would still hyperventilate when we quarreled or if I was under stress. Doug had always been accepting of my bipolar, but that still didn't make it easy for him when I would go into a bipolar cycle. The medication helped for the most part, unless I was triggered or in a very stressful situation. An episode could also happen because of a lack of sleep. I knew for years that if I didn't take proper care of myself, eat right, exercise, and get rest I could experience an episode. But when life got busy, I would forget my self-care strategies and sometimes still have episodes of mania and/or depression.

As I continue looking back, I can see that during the first six months of us being in our new house, the stress that had been beneath the surface had begun to spill over. Moving is never easy, the kids' behavior had gotten to both of us, and we had been arguing more, especially at night. Money was tight. We also spent a great deal of time helping Cooper with his homework because, as I mentioned elsewhere, he needed our patience and direction with his challenges related to Asperger's.

Doug and I each needed our own stress relievers and space. I had recently been working as a skincare consultant as a side job for fun, and I intended to make extra money. I found out that job didn't work well with my impulse control issues when it was too easy to buy the products I sold with one click. I ended up running up the balances on our credit cards because I bought a huge amount of inventory—and even extra things—with the idea that I could deduct them as business expenses. I was making some money, but not enough to cover all I had spent—not even close.

We even got audited by the IRS because they were scrutinizing home businesses at the time, and I deducted many things—even a television and a refrigerator. I was able to show receipts and justify it all. We got through the audit without harm, but Doug and I were shaken. I stopped being a consultant because of the temptation to spend money. Money had been an issue in Doug's previous marriage, so he was extra sensitive to the topic. He became more stressed with our financial situation and used working late or going out at night as his means of escape. I sensed we were beginning to grow apart.

Around that time, during the winter of 2005, I began having dreams building off the scene I had witnessed between Doug and Blair a year earlier at his fortieth birthday party. In my dreams, they were together in casual settings and locked intimate, and sometimes it felt like they were mocking me. My husband would even reject me when she was around. I would wake up in a panic.

Even if I had pushed the dreams out of the forefront of my mind, they were still in my subconscious thoughts. I would wake up and tell Doug, "I had one of my bad dreams again."

I didn't know if my dreams were a warning from God or a mind game from Satan. In retrospect, I think the Holy Spirit was telling me something was wrong. Doug had been different intimately. He either wanted to fantasize with me, or he didn't want to be close to me at all. I shared my most intimate thoughts with him to get closer to him during this time, but I was, many times, still rejected.

It wasn't just the bad dreams that were difficult; there were times in my waking hours that confirmed my worst fears. I was present at Doug's work events when Blair would flirt with Doug right in front of me. She seemed very sexually aggressive with all the men around her. She loved attention, and she was ten years younger than me. I had befriended her only because Doug wanted to do some couples' things with her and her husband. We attended a football game, went to their house, and attended those work events. I even agreed to have a party for her at her house when I was a Pampered Chef consultant when she asked me to. I didn't trust her since that long hug at Doug's milestone birthday —and everything I had witnessed since then—between her and my husband. But Doug wanted me to try to be friends with her, so I tried, though not very convincingly.

I agreed to the Pampered Chef party. I thought, *How could I say no to her idea for a party?* I had only just started at my second attempt at being a consultant again, and I was trying to earn trust from Doug by showing him that I had learned my financial lesson. I wish I could say that the party helped me be successful in my professional endeavor, but I can say that I honored my husband's request to try to get along with Blair.

I wish that he had honored me, and I wish I would have seen the writing on the wall sooner...

His work events continued that required the two of them and others to meet after hours to talk about work and build relationships with clients. I never knew when Doug would come home. He told me I was paranoid for thinking something wasn't good about these situations. He also said that there were other people around when the two of them were in a meeting, so it was no big deal. It was feeling more and more like a big deal to me. *His absence and words were contributing to my dreams*, I thought. *Or had the big green-eyed monster, jealousy, taken over, and was I being irrational like he said?* My doubts made me even more vulnerable for what would happen next.

On a sunny day in the early fall 2006, I was nearing forty-five. Doug and I were outside. I still couldn't shake the feeling that my dreams had been telling me something, and my gut feeling was more of a gnawing feeling now. I asked him point blank, "So what is really happening with you and Blair? Are you having an affair?"

I didn't expect what happened next.

Doug responded reluctantly, "Yes, I have been having an affair with her for more than a year."

My thoughts raced, *Maybe I was right all along, and it had started around the time of his party and continued.*

"What!!?? I said, More than a year!? How long really?"

121

No response.

I didn't want to believe what I had just heard...My heart dropped like an anvil and began aching. I tried not to cry, but the floodgates were open. Through my tears, I began asking more questions.

"Does her husband know? Why did you do this?"

Doug and I decided to drive around to talk more instead of letting the neighbors hear us argue outside. I was in shock and wanted to do nothing but yell and scream at the news as my anger invaded my tears and disbelief.

"What in the world are you thinking!? We are a family!"

Just then, I looked inside the console since I was now suspicious of everything. My trust was shattered completely. In the console, I discovered a letter from a Sioux Falls business, and, surprised, I asked, "What is this? Are you looking for a new job?"

He confirmed my latest fear, "Yes, I'm looking."

"What in the hell are you going to do about your family?" I said angrily.

"What about our kids and Blair's kids?"

Oh my, things had gone way too far. Why would he even apply for this job? Our family wasn't planning on moving. A move would be just for him. How could Doug and I get our marriage back?

I did not believe in divorce. My marriage vows were gospel to me, and I never believed his cheating on me with another woman could happen in my wildest dreams. *Had I been warned in my dreams for the past year and a half and just chosen to ignore what I didn't want to believe for far too long?* All I could do at that point was wish that I had acted on my underlying instincts sooner.

Either way, my world was falling apart. Though I had nightmares about the two of them together many times. I didn't think an affair would happen to me in real life! I was an eternal optimist, and I trusted my husband—even if I didn't trust her.

When we got home after our car ride, he went upstairs and began packing his suitcase.

"What in the hell is happening?" I yelled.

Silence.

"What are you doing?"

More Silence.

"I don't understand what is going on!" I was in shock, numb, and aching all at the same time. "Where are you going?" I asked as I pleaded through the tears.

I pounded on his chest, crying uncontrollably, "No, this can't be happening."

I felt completely blindsided, like I had been hit by a truck. I had just learned about their affair, and hours later, he was moving out.

Finally he said, "She and I are committed, and I'm going to live with my mother until I figure out a plan."

"What about counseling or talking through this?" I said, feeling inside desperate and deflated, as I continued to cry, now more in a panic. I became hysterical and began to hyperventilate.

He replied matter-of-factly, "I'm done. I don't want to talk anymore."

He walked out the door, and there I was, alone knowing my children would soon come home from school.

I didn't ask him to leave. I was angry, but my love didn't just go away through all the pain I felt! *What would I do? What would I tell the kids?* I wanted to figure this out...or at least have time to process what was happening! He left mere hours after his confession.

My begging and pleading could not stop him. Our children staying with me and not him could not stop him. This woman had a tight grip on my husband, and I felt like I no longer knew him.

God, what am I going to do? I realized that I had done things wrong and that we had had trouble communicating lately, but my actions hadn't warranted an affair! *Not This. Not to me. God, why did You let this happen to me? Is it because I'm flawed with my illness that he doesn't want me anymore? Has he had enough? Was it that incident with credit cards and money when I was out of control? Or is he really out of love with me?*

I told a few good friends right away, and someone at my work, to relieve the burden of this new secret everyone would soon know about.

With the bipolar causing my emotions to be unstable under stress and dealing with my husband's affair and his moving out, I was riveted into an unknown range of heightened emotions. I knew I would have to walk directly through the fire. I didn't like it, but I loved my children and job—I needed to be present for them. I had become numb, and I knew I was still in shock. I was able to keep both my job and my children—even though I didn't feel like I was performing at work or mothering at the level I wanted to.

I began my life as a single mother, except for every other weekend. Those weekends, even though I was sad about being left out, were what I needed to regain my strength to carry on. I spent needed time learning to trust God more by amping up my prayer life and asking for my marriage to be restored or my heart to be healed. I thought it was going to be up to me to seek divine help and pull myself back up. In my sobbing, at night after the kids were back with me and in bed, I found that the Holy Spirit comforted me. I now call what began to happen to me "First Aid from the Holy Spirit." It was all the comfort I had. I felt alone otherwise. I felt like the Holy Spirit was a healing balm that gave me enough strength to survive every day. And I continued to move forward, one step at a time.

Many times when I was alone, I would look at the beautiful wedding day picture in our wedding album and just cry and cry. *How did this all go so wrong? What did my future hold?*

But then, the Holy Spirit would put another layer of soothing balm onto my wounded heart in various ways. I was comforted when I heard Praise and Worship music and spending time with the triune God in prayer brought a peace that I desperately needed. I could feel a glimmer of hope.

Even though I knew I was not alone because the Holy Spirit was with me, I still had my share of setbacks. At times, I could do nothing but sleep, cry, try desperately to take care of my two children, and work part-time at my job at the school district. Although I had some good days, I was still often depressed. I knew that I was less than who I needed to be for Cooper and Olivia. Holy Spirit reassured me that I was not alone. So, while I was going through so much, I realized that it was okay to ask for help. I knew I needed support to care for my mental health and to get additional help and mentoring for my children. I found out at their school about a program called Big Brothers and Big Sisters, so I enrolled them in it. They both were assigned a mentor to spend time with them and take them to movies and activities. I wanted to ensure that they saw the world and other men and women who could provide them with fun and activity. Their sessions also gave me time alone to regroup so that I could be a good mom. This organization and the mentors my children had were truly a God-send, and the children seemed to be okay despite all that was happening. They had great teachers, mentors, and friends who made a significant impact on their lives. I learned firsthand that it takes a village to raise children.

One step forward, two steps back, it seemed. I still remember that Wednesday night during the summer of 2007 when I was forty-six and I learned that Doug had moved from his mom's to Sioux Falls to be with Blair after we separated officially. I decided that since I had been separated for almost a year, I should try to help myself and go to a divorce counseling group my therapist recommended.

I sat nervously in a circle with men and women I didn't know. It was awkward to say the least. We went systematically around the room and shared our stories. One after another, we shared our names and what brought us there. We shared the saddest, most traumatic parts of our lives. None of us could help each other; we couldn't even help ourselves. The discussion was about hard topics, but we all had one thing in common: We were simply trying to survive the loss of our dream.

Life as each of us knew it would not be the same as it had been before the extreme difficulties we had each experienced. I remember one of the counselors at the divorce group meeting told us about the five stages of grief: denial, anger, bargaining, depression, and acceptance when someone dies. He said people face the same stages with the death of a marriage. These phases sometimes come in waves together. He continued, "Separation and divorce are like death without a casserole." When I heard that phrase, it struck a nerve. I wondered, *How did my life end up here?*

I knew that I needed to try to move forward. But it was a hard process. We put our house on the market. His idea, not mine. I didn't like the idea of uprooting the children from the only home they knew. I agreed to sell because I needed some of his financial support for the kids, and I knew I had no choice but to comply at least for a while until I figured out a way to keep the house I loved. It had been my dream, and it was our home.

I desperately needed to continue to get stronger, and I continued to intentionally do my part to keep growing spiritually. I was near what I had learned was the final stage of grief: acceptance. I remember doing laundry one day, and I heard *"Take My Yoke."* I immediately looked up the following verse in the Bible, which says:

"Come to me, all you who are weary and burdened, and I will give you rest. Take my yoke upon you and learn from me, for I am gentle and humble in heart, and you will find rest for your souls. For my yoke is easy, and my burden is light"
(Matthew 11:28–30)

Why hadn't I given my doubts to God when I first had them? I thought once again. I was trying to believe God for His best outcome, but I was growing weary again from all that had transpired.

My separation went on for another six months, and eventually, it took a toll on my mental state. I was exhausted, and in August 2007, I ended up in the behavioral hospital for a week to get help because I was breaking down again emotionally with bipolar and excessive stress. My anxiety level reached a crescendo, and I was suicidal once again. I knew that I needed professional help—more counseling and extra medication—to stabilize from bipolar, to get back to normal, and to move forward. I had to get better for my children. I was afraid if we got divorced, I might lose them too. I couldn't let that happen. They were my world. But I needed rest first. The hospital stay would provide that.

That week-long hospitalization stay was a time of ups and downs. While I was there, we had a group session, and the assignment was to write a letter to Doug and "that woman." At the time, I cringed even saying her name. The idea was to get all your emotions out on paper, no matter how ugly they were, and then burn the paper. That exercise was a good thing to do because earlier in my process with Doug and his mistress, when I was so angry, I remembered driving by his office and thinking, *I hope she doesn't come out of the building when I'm driving by, or I might try to run her over.* I didn't know what I would do.

Her husband had anger too, and he had confronted Doug. The police were called to handle the situation. Eventually, Blair and her husband divorced. It was hard for me to look back at all that had happened and to realize how many lives were affected, but I needed to so that I could heal. I found that the exercises were actually helpful. According to the mental health professionals, it's a good idea to revisit the pain as you begin to heal, but it is not okay to stay in that place. Instead, they advise moving through the pain and looking toward the hope of a different future.

As I did the exercise that was recommended, my thoughts drifted back to when Doug had even given up a great job with his company that he had been at for twenty years to be with "that woman."

It was hard enough for me to deal with the infidelity, but an even more heartbreaking thought that was on repeat was, *How was all this affecting our children?* Cooper was old enough to understand a little. Olivia knew that her dad wasn't at home like he should be, but at her age, some of the situation went over her head. Doug would drive down from Sioux Falls every other weekend. He would take the kids with him even though we had no legal arrangement. I wanted the kids to feel as normal as possible, and part of that was getting to see him.

Olivia did tell me later that she thought she was going on a business trip with Daddy when she went to his apartment on the weekends. She said she would cry herself to sleep because she wanted Mommy.

More of how the kids were affected will be shared later in the book. But for now, I'm going to stay on the topic of what life was like for me.

The whole situation was so surreal. I couldn't believe what I was experiencing was my life.

I had seen a movie about an ex-husband coming back on the weekends. In the movie, he treated his kids with extravagance that his wife couldn't afford. Others in the movie called him a "Disney dad" because he took his kids to Disneyland to look like the good guy to his kids and outshine the mother.

Doug was the "Disney dad" in our lives for a while. He would come back to where the kids and I lived in Northwest Iowa, and then he would take Cooper and Olivia out for fun activities and meals while I waited anxiously for their return.

He was having fun with my kids, just like those divorced dads in the movie I had watched, and I couldn't get over feeling left out. I tried to be happy that my kids could spend time with their dad. I never wanted to jeopardize that.

A year-and-a-half after he moved out, Doug was unrecognizable to me. He had lost weight, and in his eyes, he no longer resembled the person I had married. I looked into his eyes once when we were talking about the children and thought, *Are you in there? Where is the Doug that I knew?*

Had I been this naive to think our marriage would last forever? Only God could repair what had been broken. Once we were separated, I understood that it was time to just pray for him because I could not control this situation. I believed that if Doug truly loved me and was in there somewhere, things would change, and restoration would happen.

These prayers of reconciliation were my only hope, and I asked friends to pray the same prayer. I reflected on breakups in high school, when my friends would say, "If you love something, set it free. If it comes back to you, it is yours. If it doesn't, it never was." What this expression doesn't tell you is how to set what has left you free, nor does it tell you how to find that peace. I hadn't fallen out of love with my husband, but part of me, at times, was still angry as a hornet that someone disturbed my nest.

Seeing my counselor on a regular basis had helped, which I had done since just after we officially separated. That was the same counselor who suggested that I go to a divorce group counseling session to get support, even though I wasn't yet divorced. That meeting was the one where I heard that "getting divorced was like a death without a casserole." The longer I walked through the journey I never imagined I'd be on, the more the statement rang true.

I can personally testify now that when your marriage falls apart, it is like death. Friends care, but they can only do so much. They can be a little standoffish. My situation made for uncomfortable and surface-level conversations. No one brought me funeral potatoes or chicken casserole. There was no comfort food offered. Most of "our" friends didn't even know what to do or say. I guess that reaction is similar to what happens after a death. People are afraid to say the wrong thing, so they just say something superficial and avoid talking about it. They did not want to pick sides. They loved us both.

Though it was hard for my friends, and even harder for me, it was not hard for God—He was guiding me every step of the way. As I mentioned, I had time to be still and listen to God when the kids were either with their dad or at Big Brother and Big Sisters. This time helped me begin to regain myself. I had lost who I was in the storm of the season since Doug had been gone.

There were times when I lashed out at whoever was around. But with some time and space, with the help of others when I was in the hospital and after, and with the mercy of God, I had grown in my faith. I prayed about every decision. I was actually starting to trust Him enough to get to the point that I didn't know if I wanted to hold on to hope of our marriage being reconciled anymore. When I asked that specific question, I prayed and felt the Lord telling me to let go.

Chapter Fourteen

MOVING FORWARD WITH GOD'S HELP

T he prayer of surrender that helped me accept wherever God might take me was a far cry from where I had been. From the day Doug left onward, I had, at times, driven myself crazy fighting for him and trying to figure out how to fix our marriage and to get him to come back. I might even say that I bordered on insanity, considering that a common definition of insanity is doing the same thing over and over and expecting different results. I had tried all I knew to do—I had talked to Doug, I had bargained, and I had even pleaded in my desperation to get him not to leave.

Eventually, however, God helped make it clear to me that it was time for me to stop fighting for him. I had always known that marriage is a two-way street, and I began to see that I was the only one working for reconciliation. As I mentioned in the last chapter, by the fall of 2007, I could feel the presence and healing of the Holy Spirit being active in my soul.

I believed He had helped plant the thought in my head: *If Doug wanted us in his life, he needed to fight for us.* I needed to get stronger for my children. I had been talking to a lawyer, but he refused to get a lawyer for himself. I felt that Doug needed to step up, whether it was finishing the divorce process or realizing what truly mattered in his life—his family. I turned it all over to God, I was doing what it said in one of Doug's grandma's favorite songs, "trust and obey, for there's no other way."

In the winter of 2008, Doug and I agreed to meet for lunch in Sioux Falls. I served him with divorce papers at that lunch. Doug seemed surprised that I had taken charge, but I was done fighting for him. I needed to stay steady and follow God's leading and to rest in the arms of my heavenly Father for all things in the future. My children and my faith had become my biggest priorities. I knew that I needed to be in a good state of mind for my children. I had prayed for our marriage; I prayed for Doug, and I even prayed for the other couple involved and their children. I knew prayer was powerful, and it was all I could do. I think I was trying to accept that I might be a single mother to these children. And I knew I had to do more than accept it—I had to take tangible steps to begin to move forward.

I got ready for bed that night several hours after Doug and I had met for lunch, realizing that alone I couldn't restore my marriage, but God could do it! I had hoped that my prayers would be answered. I prayed for His will to be done in our marriage as I prayed the Lord's prayer. My children and I deserved a more stable life. We were important. I read a portion of Psalm 46 in my Bible as I sat quietly, thinking of what the future might hold:

> "God is our refuge and strength, an ever-present help in trouble.
> Therefore we will not fear, though the earth give way
> and the mountains fall into the heart of the sea,
> though its waters roar and foam
> and the mountains quake with their surging
> (Psalm 46:1–3)

I let go once again and let God have his way in my life. *He knew best,* I thought. I thought of another favorite verse, Ephesians 3:20, which promises that He would bless me exceedingly, abundantly, above all that I can ask or think.

I embraced my relationship with my triune God even more. I whispered to myself as I drifted off to sleep, but with God, all things are possible (see Matthew 19:26).

I started to believe this promise more and more over time. Now, looking back, I can testify that as we turn everything over to Him, truly all things are possible. I had always felt this verse was true for other people, but as I prayed over my situation, I had hope that it could become true for my family too.

As 2008 continued, we continued talking and interacting. *God was showing His faithfulness to my prayers,* I thought. After much discussion and sorrowful hearts on both our parts for what had happened to us, Doug decided to take a new job in Hull to be closer to us all and to prove that he had a change of heart. He had hopes of reentering our family's life.

Though he was very remorseful, this arrangement and talks of him moving back in were not without stipulations: I laid down the law and said he could not attend evening work activities unless I knew who would be there, and we would commit to having open communication about our feelings. We also agreed not to fight over money and to be a godly husband and wife to each other. I put a saying over our bed, "Always Kiss Me Goodnight," and we agreed to never again go to bed angry or with unresolved issues.

We both had regrets and guilt about that hard season in our marriage. We wished it had never happened, but it did. We would learn the lessons that it gave us and be wiser for it. There were many lessons to rehash, and it took endless effort.

I had regrets from before he left about my impulsive spending periods. I also felt shame that I had been so blind to what was going on with Doug. Even when I sensed there were problems, I tried to handle them myself or push them down for far too long. I wish I had turned everything over to God right away.

Doug will share his regrets in his own words later in the book.

But for now, I'll continue to share where we were headed in leveling our lives with God's peace not only with an underlying mental illness but also facing the often fatal wound of infidelity. We faced a long road of forgiveness and grace. I was in the process of forgiving but not forgetting. It was hard to not be triggered by things like him looking at his phone or getting home late. Learning to trust him, while at the same time safeguarding myself from further hurt with the very real possibility of him cheating again, was a very delicate balance. Trust was and is something that had to be earned—for me or for any spouse coming to the reconciliation table after infidelity. As Doug reentered our lives, I could see he was working with all his heart to regain that trust.

We started couples counseling and took divorce off the table. The counselor that we went to had counseled me during our separation, so she knew our entire story. She was very gracious to invite Doug into our sessions. Later, we both did some counseling on our own. I went to my counselor, and he went to a different counselor who was recommended to him.

We both continued individual therapy, and we also met with a good friend who became a Christian life coach. We did sessions separately and together. We learned it was essential to put God first even before each other but also to let Him walk with us in our everyday life together. She helped us to understand more about biblical marriage roles. And eventually, she helped more firmly weave those responsibilities into the fabric of our lives.

She helped us call to mind two verses from Ephesians that were used in our wedding and became meaningful during our reconciliation. Even today as I write and looking forward, they serve as a reminder of our vows to each other with God and our renewed commitment to each other:

> *"Husbands, love your wives, just as Christ loved the church…*
> *For this reason a man will leave his father and mother and be*
> *united to his wife, and the two will become one flesh"*
> (Ephesians 5:25, 31).

If you are struggling in your marriage and you would like to learn more about biblical roles of spouses, I recommend that you do an Internet search on Bible verses about marriage. You can also seek books and resources about rebuilding a Christian marriage after an affair. My point as I introduce these concepts in this chapter is to simply tell you that if both parties are willing, with God's help, you can get through an affair.

Through counseling during our process of reconciliation, I took away three things:

1. Healing takes time.

2. Success is dependent on both parties having God's love and respect as they walk through life together.

3. Sharing how we feel is key because miscommunications can bring back hurt that remains.

Overall, I learned that forgiveness and communication are at the core of everything of re-establishing "normal" in a biblical and healthy way for all parties. These two action steps are foundational for all human relationships—and those who face the challenge of mental illness are no exception.

We found that we needed to have an acknowledgment of what transpired, along with a newfound grace on all fronts as we worked to forgive each other. We also became keenly aware of how this separation and indiscretion had affected the kids by the way they would react or be sad if we had arguments after we started living together after our separation. They had definitely been affected by it all even though they seemed resilient. When a trauma occurs in a marriage, it affects everyone in the family. Healing is important. It is also necessary for all of us to trust one another as we move forward.

As I reflect on the long and painful season, I recognize that healing isn't about erasing the past. It's about allowing God to redeem it. A journey from betrayal to reconciliation to restoration was not instant. It was filled with setbacks but as we learned, the time was anointed. In quiet moments of surrender, tear-filled prayers and sometimes moment-by-moment choices to trust again, we found a new beginning. Not perfect by any stretch, but real and rooted in His grace.

But my voice is just one part of this story.

As with any story, there is more to tell because healing never happens in a vacuum. Others around you are always affected. Doug has his own story to share. His regrets, repentance, and the slow, intentional rebuilding of trust. Our children, Cooper and Olivia, walked with us through this valley too. They saw the brokenness, felt the pain, and witnessed the repair. All three of them will share their perspective and journey later in this book.

As I wrap up the overall story of our reconciliation, my biggest take away was to have one honest conversation and one prayer at a time...As we sought and found one piece at a time, we discovered that God's promises are true: He will not leave nor forsake us, He works all things for good, and He has great plans for our future.

After we started our journey as a family again living in the same home, one of the pieces God led me to was deeper self-reflection. That piece, as I would soon learn, was critical to my ongoing healing process.

Chapter Fifteen

TAKING RESPONSIBILITY

During the reconciliation process, and despite the ongoing emotional struggles with trust issues and having bipolar, I was still challenged to take ownership for my actions. This sort of responsibility meant I had to go back and figure out why these things happened and do my part to become better. I learned and accepted that bipolar wasn't an excuse for my poor behavior, nor was it my identity. My God-given identity as Teresa didn't have anything to do with the illness. My identity in Christ was as a beloved daughter, and I would need to learn to embrace that role.

I began to sift through my emotions during the healing process. Toni, my alter ego, couldn't help smooth things out even when learning new ways to act was hard. As I have shared, she had morphed in my difficult seasons into a harsh protector—even a bully. She no longer made me look good. In fact, she did just the opposite.

Prior to my separation, though, I had been able to keep most of my emotional outbursts within the confines of my home. However, with the stress of the affair and beyond, I was no longer able to choose the time or place my emotions flared.

Though I was trying hard to control all the emotions, I couldn't forget the many times during our marriage troubles, separation, and early reconciliation timeframe from 2004 to 2008 when I was cruel both to others and myself.

An incident in 2007 that I have a hard time forgetting was when I responded impatiently to a co-worker, "Do I have to do your job for you!" I immediately regretted what I had done, realizing this person had simply asked for my help but wasn't quick to understand what I was explaining. I then understood that I was stressed beyond my ability to control my emotions and anger. The co-worker just wanted help from me, but I was not capable of helping anyone when an anger outburst came.

Another time early in our reconciliation in 2008, I had just had rotator cuff surgery, and I stormed into the appliance store and told them they needed to get me a different repair person because the current one couldn't fix my dishwasher. Before I was done, I had F-bombed the person at the counter and recommended the repairman should be fired for his incompetence. These examples weren't the first or last times that I would lash out at whoever was in my path during my time of extreme life difficulties and subsequent healing seasons.

I remember one moment clearly at the grocery store when I realized I was doing exactly what I was sad about my mom doing when I was young. She used to lose it and was harsh in the grocery store checkout line because she was struggling with undiagnosed bipolar. I would just walk away because I wanted to get away from the situation quickly. At the time, I would get angry because she embarrassed me, but later, when I was doing similar things, I realized that maybe her hormones, bipolar disorder, and stress had brought out these things in her like they did in me.

I can see looking back that I was responding like a bear. I would have been wise to hibernate instead of going out. I cringe when I think about my reactions. I was angry and my words were harsh. My emotions were hopping all over the place, and I just couldn't control them. Cutting statements would come out of my mouth, and as soon as they came out, I wished that I could put them back in. These outbursts were such a large struggle for me.

To this day, I cannot single out one cause for these outbursts because there were many. Before, during, and after the separation and reconciliation, I was also experiencing migraines and early menopause on top of bipolar disorder.

As I started perimenopause, I became even more aware of other women who had challenges with extreme traumas like divorce with changing hormones. I had always been a "feeler," and God had enabled me to sense distress in others. I could also see that hormones were likely affecting them adversely because I was experiencing the same shifts.

Because I was more in tune with others' emotions, their actions affected me. It was as if I was taking on their burdens emotionally, and doing so affected my own moods.

When I was working within the school system, I began seeing young people who looked like they were beginning to show signs that they could be bipolar. The difficult part was that I felt burdened by their issues, which weighed me down even more. My desire was to help the kids; I began asking myself how I could possibly help these kids. My empathy stirred a desire and planted a seed to help others who were struggling with their emotions that they could not control. At the time, I shared those thoughts with Doug and a few others, but mostly I kept them to myself because I didn't think I had anything of enough value to share since I wasn't a licensed therapist. This book is the fruit of that seed that God first planted all those years ago. I would have several more years of healing growth before God would make it clear that I was ready to help others, though.

In retrospect, I see that in the first few years after Doug moved in, I wasn't trusting my friends enough to invite them to get close to me, and I was definitely still relearning trust with Doug. I wondered if I had really ever trusted anyone besides Grandma. I continued to build up an emotional fortress. The walls protected me, but they also kept others out.

Because I still had scars from the near demise of my marriage, I realized I was dealing with the fear of abandonment. My rampant thoughts exhausted me both physically and emotionally.

I was almost paranoid, thinking about what others might be saying about me in their heads. Or worse, I thought that they might be talking about me behind my back. These assumptions from not trusting others were always just under the surface. Silly things would irritate me inside, and I would get angry at times for no real reason. This irritation was my internal problem; I was creating issues in my mind that weren't really there.

I could tell myself that my assumptions were not reality; they were my perceptions through a skewed lens because of all I was going through. But they still stumped me at times and felt real.

I didn't help my problems when I engaged in self-sabotage by putting myself down verbally. I had practiced a victim mentality since the time I was around nine or ten years old, and I continued to use that tactic in my marriage and with other close friendships. I think I did it because of my hope that other people would feel sorry for me and direct more attention my way.

I did get more attention because people would try to compliment me as a way of trying to help me feel better. I, however, didn't accept the compliments. I turned the positive comments into negative words I said about myself, which, also in retrospect, I can see had to be frustrating. In fact, my responses eventually drove people away because no one likes to hear others putting themselves down repeatedly.

The worst part was that I realized that I could be causing others difficulty with my trauma—or so I thought. I have since learned that others are responsible for how they take on what another person says, and, with the exception of my immediate family, they likely weren't thinking about my words as much as I thought they were. What I did understand at the time was that they seemed to be growing weary of my behavior—and so was I.

At one point, I eventually asked friends that we used to do things with why we were no longer included in gatherings or trips.

One person gave me a little insight on who was invited and who wasn't when she said, "We need to feel comfortable with the same couples we spend time with and steer clear of those who we don't always feel comfortable with." I deduced from that, *Doug and I don't make our friends comfortable anymore.*

145

I cried at hearing this because I knew the person who said this wasn't the only person who felt that way. As my relationships with friends changed over time, I wondered, *Was it Doug and my separation they are steering away from, or was it my bipolar diagnosis?*

It was in that moment that I realized my raging emotions had caught up with me, and things would not be the same. I knew I had work to do, but I wasn't yet able to determine how to accomplish it.

In addition to struggling with bipolar, and then hormonal shifts, I had always been a very emotional and sensitive person—those qualities tend to go along with being a "feeler." Even a person's tone and demeanor could trigger me. With my emotions as intense as they were, I was often prone to debate a topic I felt passionate about. Because I was negative to others and blew up at small frustrations, I would have regret. Afterwards, I would criticize and judge myself with negative self-talk. I hated that I had turned my inner turmoil outward and lashed out more at others.

In the years leading up to turning fifty, I developed a greater understanding of what I had done. I saw that bipolar and hormones augmented the severity of my behaviors.

I took a look in the mirror to take the log out of my own eye as Jesus instructs us to do in Matthew 7:3–5. I stopped blaming Doug, my parents, and friends for my struggles. Blaming others was what I had done often up to that point to protect myself from some hard truths that I had been pushing down inside me.

I saw that I was really dissatisfied with how my own life was progressing being separated, changing hormonally, and then attempting to put something back together that had been shattered by broken trust. My emotions were like a snowball that just kept collecting and collecting and rolling and rolling, getting bigger and harder to manage all the time. Then, as I looked at what I created, it was like the snowball was ready to roll over who I had hoped to become. I couldn't get out of my own way, because I just kept adding fuel to the fire, or adding snow to the snowball.

The tension just kept building, and I kept trying to push the tension forward along with me. Even though the snowball wanted to roll downhill, it was as if I was trying to push an ever-increasingly-bigger snowball uphill. It was a battle just to get to the next day when I would struggle with depression because of all I was dealing with. Suicidal thoughts would still come into the forefront in times of difficulty even though I knew better how to fight them by that point. Praying, "God please help me," did help. But, I was tired all the time, and I was still not healed from my past and recent life traumas.

One step forward two steps back was my way of living. Through it all, I knew that to get to a better life, I would need fortitude to go through the muck and mire to get to the beautiful.

I remember Grandma saying, "Having something good never comes easy. But, that is why it's worth having because you work for it." So I pressed on.

By 2015, at fifty-four, nine years after Doug initially left, I was still doing therapy and was also engaging in some life coaching with my friend, who I mentioned in the last chapter. I not only still needed help to rebuild my marriage in a healthy way by implementing the practices she had taught us, but I also needed to apply what she was teaching me to have healthy friendships.

I had to look inside even more to work on my contributions to my relationships with other family members and friends. My dear friend who was a Christian life coach was God's choice for that role because she knew me well, and she was trained to help in that area. She not only gave me practical tips but also she reminded me God was *for* me, and so were my other friends; they just weren't equipped to handle me sometimes. In addition, she helped me realize that friends were really for me when they could be.

My life coach also pointed out example after example in the Bible of God's love, and she helped me see all the blessings in my own life so I could recognize how much God loved me. The reason we started with God's love was because that needed to be the foundation for all of my relationships. I had to know I was loved, and I needed to love myself before I could be a good friend, mother, and spouse. I learned His love is really key to healthy relationships. I discovered loving others starts with God and me.

Why had I let life rob me of this truth, when my grandmother had modeled it so well? I wasn't sure. All I can tell you is that undergoing life coaching was so helpful for me to continue my healing journey.

Part of the recovery process included making a list of behaviors I wish I could change: emotional outbursts in public, mood swings, and blaming my bipolar for my actions instead of taking personal responsibility.

Looking back, I can see that healing happens in layers. Nearly a decade after life coaching, I had to more closely examine what happened that brought me to where I am as I write this book. Prior to starting this book, I thought my suicide attempt incident when I was twenty-four was the most difficult event of my life. But actually, the road to forgiveness, reconciliation, and restoration after my crumbling marriage was harder and longer.

As I've shared, the separation and near demise of my marriage, contributed to a domino effect of trouble, and it is a time that I wanted to forget and never revisit. I learned in therapy, however, that God uses the hard times in life to cultivate lessons worth learning and passing on. Healing remains an ongoing process, but with every look back or with every examination of the present, greater peace and revelation emerges.

So, before I move on to what happened after our reconciled life was completely settled, I'm going to go back one more time to share how I took responsibility to more fully trust Doug and God. I needed to let go of what was most necessary to live as my true self—my alter ego.

In retrospect, I can see that after Doug reentered our family many years earlier, I neglected re-establishing close ties with him as a result of my lack of trust.

I put my children first. I guess that was more because of the trauma and mothering instinct. I had put the kids first for so long during our time of difficulty that it was hard to shift gears and put Doug first again.

That's why we had both decided to do life coaching separately at first to work on being a godly husband and wife to each other first and foremost. The intimate connection between God and each of us needed to be reestablished to help us as individuals with God's divine direction before we could reconnect intimately with each other.

You don't just snap your fingers to heal a relationship even after you forgive. Doug and I discussed how forgiveness is easier when we don't immediately assume the worst about the other person. As I have also shared, remembering blessings and practicing gratitude about Doug became crucial to forgiving and accepting each other's shortcomings.

As I grew in my understanding about how to have close relationships, I learned that I could only control my actions and responses—not the other person involved.

My life coach also helped me understand that sometimes to avoid an outburst, it would be best to remove myself from situations during times of overwhelming emotions. Taking her advice and removing myself helped me focus on what I could control.

Another essential practice for the safeguarding of my marriage was taking care of myself by managing stress, eating well, and getting proper rest. Approaching recovery with the best intentions and a positive mindset is also key.

By implementing all these strategies, my coach helped me realize that I could build mental resilience and effectively bounce back from challenging situations in my marriage.

One of our greatest challenges arose because of a habit that I had developed and used to cope since before Doug and I met. As I stated earlier, when I started understanding that I had chemical changes in my brain when I was diagnosed bipolar at almost twenty-five, I decided to say to myself that during my depressed days and manic days, "Toni is here." It was because I had to fake my way to feeling okay. Then, when I calmed and relaxed enough to feel better, tell myself "Teresa is back."

I had shared with Doug how I used Toni as an alternate persona to help me in times of trouble. He was the only person besides my therapist that knew that I had invited Toni into my life, and eventually it became a point of almost humor with Doug and I because trust me, in dealing with bipolar, sometimes you need to laugh at yourself to survive.

He would say something like, "Glad you're back, Teresa. Toni can be a real pain."

I really wanted just to be the old Teresa with her normal faults. This negative way of coping had turned into much more than the glamorized acting and having fun as a child. In fact, it was not acting at all. When I was Toni during my late forties, the chemicals in my brain would get triggered in ways I still don't totally understand, and it was like all hell would break loose like with that massive snowball I described earlier.

As I have mentioned, Toni became aggressive and lashed out at others because of my illness, and not just because of the stress or trauma I was currently experiencing. She was reacting to all the hurts I had experienced in my life. Toni would hurt others before they could hurt her. The problem always was that this other part of me was living inside my body, and all the outside world could see was Teresa. I'm sure, just like my husband, people wished I would have acted more like I used to.

151

Out of love for my children and because of my gratitude to God, the time came when I knew I needed to be completely Teresa—the best version of Teresa that God had intended when He created me. My family deserved the real authentic me. When I had that thought, I also thought, *Was it time to get rid of Toni altogether, or did I need her?*

My therapist said, "You need to let her go, and just keep that part of her that is your own self-confidence."

How do I do that? I have no idea how to separate the two. Do I have my own confidence as simply Teresa? I thought. But I needed to let Toni go and to become my true self—whatever that looked like.

Relying on putting up a false front was exhausting, and I knew doing so would even threaten my mental health more if I were to continue relying on Toni. After I had gone through more forgiveness with Doug, I knew I needed to be the best I could be for him as well. I had intentionally spent time destressing and spending time by myself with God for healing. I would no longer try to please or entertain; I would deal with situations intentionally but naturally. Taking responsibility and being authentically Teresa was the goal—and the hope for my new normal.

Chapter Sixteen

DEPENDING ON GOD AND GIVING UP BAD COPING MECHANISMS

Through a few more stories, I will tell you how I set out to make the rest of my life as the best of my life. Pain without progress on my part would have left me still in pain. Rebuilding with God is worth all the effort, and the way God uses our pain for His good and ours is truly amazing.

First, I had to address my bad coping mechanisms. I had developed many including faking my way through life with Toni, putting myself down to get compliments, and pushing everything down and not dealing with it. But the worst of these was Toni. So it was obvious at this point that I needed to focus on getting rid of my persona of Toni from elementary school days and beyond. As I have mentioned, she had stuck with me over the years in my bag of tricks to pull out when I needed her. But I still wondered, *Did I really need her?* She had gotten out of control, and she seemed to come out more like one of my bipolar moods.

I really had to take a deep dive into why I had looked to Toni as a means of surviving. With a therapist, we realized that Toni was trying to protect me. Part of her was because of my illness and mood swings, and part of her was because of all the hurts I had experienced. I learned that Toni was really not a healthy part of my life when my therapist said I had borderline personality disorder. She told me that I would need to create healthy habits and boundaries for myself to recover from this crutch.

The problem always was that Toni was another part of me and was living inside my body, and all the outside world could see was Teresa being harsh and dysfunctional. I'm sure, just like my husband, people wished I would have acted more like I used to.

I learned that Toni was a bad coping mechanism that I integrated in my life first by choice and later by habit. Although I had seen using Toni had backfired, it was difficult to hear from a mental health professional that by using her, I had actually engaged in further self-sabotaging my mental health. Acknowledging the truth, however, was the first step. This realization gave me the courage to look inside and do whatever it took to become my true self.

As my therapist had said, I needed to say goodbye to Toni. I knew that it was the only way to move forward with a new self, the me God intended all along.

Despite knowing this was the right thing to do, I was still hesitant, however, to not use her because she had been my protector and false front for so long. My doctors, my therapist, and my nudging from God reassured me that she had more than served her purpose. My therapist also helped when she said I could think of her as retired—and that the best parts of Toni could be integrated into my true self in a more positive way.

I knew that the harsh side of her had no place in my life anymore. I was ready to start to let her go—with the help of my therapist. To begin the process, my therapist had me pretend that I was lying down, and to envision a safety net under me. That net would be there, no matter what. That safety net, she explained, is God protecting you. Then she said, "Now relax and let all the stress in your body go." This visualization reminded me of progressive relaxation I had done in the past, but because we had invited God into the scene, it felt more secure and peaceful. The safety net helped me repeat after her and say, "God has my back." After that session, I had some homework to do.

I did some mirror activities, during which I would talk kindly to myself, saying, "Teresa, you are enough."

I continued those words with," You are enough. People love you. God loves you."

I knew I would need to tell Toni as I looked at myself in the mirror that I did not need her anymore. Then I remembered my therapist's words. "The good and healthy parts of her can stay, but they must come out as the true Teresa, calm, relaxed, and authentic to her soul and heart."

It was time. I had to say the hard part myself.

Looking in the mirror, trembling, I said, "Toni, I don't need you anymore."

I took a breath.

"I am going to be okay." I continued, "God loves me and always has."

I took another breath.

"Though it is hard to let you go, I need to say goodbye."

Tears started to form and rolled down my cheeks. I sensed that the part of me that was so familiar with Toni was sad, and I suppose I was too. It was goodbye, after all, and still a loss of what I had relied on.

"I will take the best qualities of you and enable them to be part of me, but the rest of you has to go."

That day, I walked out of my bathroom a different person. I had decided that from then on, I would live without Toni—I had to make that conscious decision. And I had to stick to it.

For many months after that, I also needed to engage in positive self-talk in the mirror and relaxing and being calm and still with God. Finally, only my true self looked back and talked back. I had become just Teresa, who was mostly calm and gentle, but with a healthy confidence. A key statement that I still say to myself in the mirror and remind myself with sticky notes is, "Just be yourself—just be authentic to how God created you, Teresa— you are enough."

Saying goodbye to Toni wasn't the only piece of the puzzle I needed to deal with to find normal. I still needed additional help to deal with my tendency to lash out at times. I reread and internalized the Book of James, and particularly Chapter 5, about the taming of the tongue. Other verses were helpful as well. I also turned to reading books, breathing, and prayer. Piece by piece, God was guiding me to gain greater clarity and greater confidence as my true self. Even if my emotions or stress attempted to throw off my equilibrium, God was beginning to show me how He was going to rearrange my life as He leveled my mind.

Chapter Seventeen

GOING BEYOND NORMAL BY GOING DEEPER WITH GOD

Our family continued to adjust to living under the same roof, which was a struggle for the next five to ten years. Many days, it was still one step forward, two steps back. As I said, I no longer used the mask of Toni. I was determined to do my best as Teresa, and I was committed to asking God often how to manage life, marriage, and family. I was committed to persist by doing even more hard work on myself. I began a process to reconstruct my life. As I did this, without my crutch of Toni, I noticed that some of the drama was starting to quiet down. I started to ask myself: *What is my (Teresa's) future?*

As I navigated my fifties, I still hoped to find a more stable and lengthier sense of "normal," which to me, still meant being like everyone else, settled with a relatively stable marriage and family.

The weight of the betrayal in my marriage, however, still fragmented my efforts and my heart. Doug's affair left an indelible mark even many years later, and I could no longer hide the shattered pieces oozing out of me. I realized I needed to reach greater levels of healing, especially to get past the fear of

157

abandonment and the unforgiveness that were still plaguing me at times.

For years, I had suppressed painful memories or leaned on Toni instead of moving forward. I was committed to stop hiding and begin rebuilding, not just for me but for my family. Though it would take years, I started investigating other interesting helpful layers of my life, noticing even the smallest details. I started to look closer at interesting and personal ways God had always communicated with me as well as examining some of the new special messages He was giving me. He prompted me to begin to pay closer attention to my dreams and recurring signs like songs, numbers, and memories that tugged at my heart.

Despite the excitement I had as I looked closer at new subjects about how God was leading me to reinvent my life in a new season, self-sabotage and doubt were still just under the surface.

I kept wondering, *What if I lose Doug again?* I didn't know if I could bear it.

These inner voices were relentless…

"What if…"

"What if…"

God, in His mercy, merged my old struggles with my greater awareness of how He uniquely communicates with me. One day, as I was driving alone, I heard the words "You're My little girl" by Go Fish sung on the radio. Tears streamed down my face because in all the aftermath of trauma, I had forgotten who loved me unconditionally and who had my back. That moment reset my soul— reminding me that God's love had to come first, and if I held onto that, I would be okay.

Songs, movies, books, and memories have always helped me process life. During my early fifties, they became a lifeline. I started to focus on what makes me who I am on the road to accepting all of me. I turned the mirror toward myself to learn more about what my mind was telling me. The first part of my mind that I wanted to take a closer look at because it fascinated me so much was my dream life. Because I am a dreamer, both at night and in envisioning my future, I wanted to understand those subconscious messages.

DREAMS AND THE HOUSE WITH MANY ROOMS

I knew I wasn't alone in this quest. Dreams and dream interpretation are recorded in the Bible, including in the story of Joseph. Joseph's dreams were symbolic, and he became an interpreter for others' dreams. He believed the interpretations came from God. The first questions I wanted to know more about were: *Why did I sometimes have a good dream and other times have nightmares? Why do I dream the same things again and again?*

I don't know when my most prevalent recurring dream started; it seems like it has always been a part of me. In this dream is a white, grand mansion with many rooms. It is big, beautiful, and inviting on the outside with a sprawling lawn. The landscaping is meticulous, as if someone is solely devoted to its care. The mansion, at the end of a long, winding road with a circular driveway in front, is the kind of house that people would notice and want to see inside. On the main floor, chandeliers and marble steps led into a ballroom. A host of strange things are going on all over the other floors in the house. Extravagant and beautiful rooms are right next to chaotic rooms, and strangers were milling around, some with familiar faces. The attic is filled with beautiful treasures; the basement is cluttered with broken things. Over the years, variations of this dream seemed to come during the most stressful seasons of my life.

Through resources like DreamBible.com[11] and DreamDictionary.org[12] and Barbie Breathitt's *A to Z Dream Symbology Dictionary*,[13] I learned that biblically, the house represents a person. The mansion was me. I concluded that the outside seemed welcoming because I learned to hide my vulnerable side, but inside, I reflected the chaos I felt living with bipolar disorder, fear, and stress.

The attic symbolized my hopes, dreams, and abilities. The basement reflected subconscious struggles—shame, depression, and unresolved trauma. As I grew older, the dream shifted, and the stairs to the attic were impassable. I wanted desperately to reach the treasures again, but I felt locked out. The interpretations were clear: I was holding myself back, locking myself out of God's potential because of fear and self-sabotage. As I learned about dreams during my fifth decade of life, *I needed to accept myself and open that door for the sake of my future*, I thought.

SIGNS, NUMBERS, AND HOLY SPIRIT GUIDANCE

Around the same time that I was investigating my dreams, I began noticing the number 444—again, and again. On clocks. On receipts. On social media. When I looked it up, I found that it symbolized guidance and protection, representing stability, structure, and balance.[14] These were all characteristics of life that I longed for.

Books became another way God spoke to me and taught me about how He was shaping my future. When I read *The Shack*, by William Paul Young,[15] it gave me a fresh vision of God's triune nature, meeting me in my pain and showing His love. It was transformative as it looked at the triune God in this out of the box interpretation. It made it more real for me. Papa or Father God was the caring parent with unconditional love that Mac needed. God was first portrayed as a woman because Mac had trouble with his own father. Jesus was portrayed as a gentle patient carpenter and Holy Spirit knew every tear shed and was a wisp of refreshing air. But they were three in one when it came to knowledge of one's life and journey. It was one of the quickest books I ever read because I couldn't put it down.

I was excited to find books about the number four, since that number had become important to me. The book on that topic that I want to mention is *The Four Agreements* by Don Miguel Ruiz. Though not a Christian book, its truths helped me retrain my thinking and live with greater peace. In addition to reading the Word each day, I found that the following four agreements mentioned in *The Four Agreements* gave me simple but profound wisdom that I could apply daily:

1. Be impeccable with your word.
2. Don't take anything personally.
3. Don't make assumptions.
4. Always do your best.

The book also showed me that I had to "come into agreement" with the things I wanted in my life before the changes would take place.[16] These four principles inspired me to move forward and gave me a simple plan of how to begin. I would even go as far as to say these principles were life-altering once I chose to apply them, which I soon did.

Another influential book I found was *The Four Cardinal Virtues*, originally credited to Plato, one of the fathers of classical philosophy. These virtues include prudence (wisdom in making right decisions), temperance (self-control and balance), fortitude (courage to endure trials), and justice (fairness, respect, and giving others their due).[17]

THE FOUR PILLARS OF LIVING B.O.L.D.

I adopted these four virtues and created an acronym and refer to them as The Four Pillars to a balanced life. God downloaded this framework to me after four decades of searching. I use the acronym B.O.L.D to explain them:

- **B**eholding Prudence: Self-awareness to pinpoint areas to work on. *Prudence* is the ability to discern the right course of action. It is then applied to real life.

- **O**bedient Temperance: Bridging the gap, having mindfulness, and diving into the Fruit of the Spirit to work on a "new self." *Temperance* is the practice of moderation and self-restraint.

- **L**oving Fortitude: Putting on the armor, feeding the soul, and accepting healing through First aid from the Holy Spirit. *Fortitude* is the courage to face difficulties and persevere.

162

- **D**ue Justice: Reaching Awareness, peace, respect, accepting and giving forgiveness, and feeling joy. *Justice* is living fairly and acting with righteousness.

These pillars are the basis for being aware and monitoring behavior. They helped me to maintain virtue and integrity in my soul and live **B.O.L.D.**ly.

As I became more self-aware through these four pillars and what they stand for, I became a better person. I practiced self-restraint and awareness in my relationships and moved the values of perseverance and character up to the top of my to do list. It really is no different than to say, "What would Jesus do?" He possessed these qualities and was the greatest role model. My faith gave me the commitment to foster the fruit of the Spirit in myself, and that has made all the difference.

FINDING MY TRUE NORMAL

As I enter my sixties, I look back with gratitude. The house dream has faded, but the lessons remain. "Normal" is not a destination. It is not about looking put together from the outside, but about living authentically, in God's presence, day by day. I spent four decades struggling to find identity, purpose, and true joy. When I found this framework and did the work, I gained balance. This time of reflection also reignited my desire and hope to help others.

I believe there was a reason that I kept seeing the numbers, hearing the songs, and paying attention to my dreams. I am glad I did because these God nudges gave me, four agreements, four pillars, and four decades (which together represents 444, my special number) that led me to where I am today in my sixties.

During the last four decades, I learned that we have control of some aspects of our life and others we do not. We all have to do our best to level our mind with God. The only things we can control are our responses and routines. I no longer strive to appear "normal," in the sense of living in a way that matches what appears normal for everyone else or in culture. Instead, I choose to create my normal with God by living according to the **B.O.L.D.** framework He gave me. Doing so empowers me to trust God's protection, His healing, and His love as He continues transforming me into greater wholeness and into the Teresa He had in mind when He created me. Well into my season of living fully, I started intentionally and repeatedly giving God the reins to follow His lead in becoming healthier in mind, body, and spirit. I would learn that these three components, at times, experience threats in one way or another, and I would soon experience a threat I hadn't gone through before.

C̦hapter E̦ighteen

LEARNING NOT TO TAKE LIFE FOR GRANTED

G etting older can be challenging, but it can also be rewarding with more time and resources to do what you love. When Doug and I had been married nearly thirty years, we were empty nesters, and we wanted a special place to relax. We established a home away from home in 2018 in a mobile home area at Lake Okoboji, which is known as the Iowa Great Lakes, and about seventy miles from our home in Orange City.

On a particular weekend, four years later, when I was sixty-one, on Saturday, August 27, 2022, to be exact, we were boating with friends. It was a beautiful, sunny, and calm day on the water. We were laughing and enjoying fun conversation with our friends. In retrospect, I am so grateful for that peaceful day. God knew I would need it.

After we got home the next day and had our evening meal, Doug and I were watching "Beat Bobby Flay" on Food Network, and I got up for a bathroom break. Within seconds of reaching the bathroom, I had excruciating pain in my head. I have had headaches before, but this was the worst one I ever had—and I had previously experienced two concussions and ongoing migraines. My pain tolerance was usually high, but I knew in my soul, body, and head that this was different than any past pain.

I walked from the bathroom where the pain started out into the living room holding my head and crying. "Oh my God, what is happening?" I said, worried.

Doug looked up, concerned. "Are you okay? Should we go to the ER?"

I had been perfectly fine just minutes before, but the intensity of my pain was overwhelming.

Without speaking, I walked to the car, holding my head, and lay down in the backseat of the car, indicating to him that the answer was *"YES, let's go to the ER."*

I thought, *God, don't let this be the end.* I prayed the Lord's Prayer in my mind, and I asked for His help for both of us. *My head is going to explode,* I thought. I could feel the pressure building in the front of my head. I could hear myself making desperate crying sounds, but I didn't care who heard me. I could tell on the way to the emergency room that Doug was also scared, which scared me even more. This was an uncharted territory. I had gotten all too familiar with hospitals over the years with bipolar episodes and depression, but this physical pain was different.

We got to the emergency room entrance. After that, the rest of my memories are a blur. Doug later told me I was vomiting and my blood pressure was off the charts from the pain. The doctors and nurse began attending to me right away.

Doug helped fill in the blank spots in my memory. After getting some pain meds for me and doing a scan of my head, we learned that I had experienced a brain hemorrhage, and my brain was bleeding internally, which put pressure on my skull. My diagnosis was a subarachnoid hemorrhage, which caused the bleeding. No one really knew why it came on so instantly.

They put me on fentanyl, but I was still in pain. I also had extreme sensitivity to light and sound. They told Doug that our ER in Orange City called for air transport to airlift me to the Sioux Falls hospital ICU. I was in and out of awareness at times because of the pain meds.

I woke up briefly when I was being rolled on a gurney to the waiting helicopter and the whirling sound. I also remember being in the helicopter for just a second when one of the EMT staff put headphones on me to drown out the sound of the engine. I knew the medical personnel were talking, but I wasn't sure what they said. The pain meds must have kicked in because I went unconscious. I don't remember anything else about the flight or arriving at the ICU.

The next thing I remember is waking up in the ICU of the hospital with Doug in my room. The medical staff was trying to get me to answer questions.

"What is your name?"

"Teresa Brunsting," I winced in pain.

"When is your birthday?"

"December 19,1961," I said, again wincing.

"Who is the president?"

"Joe Biden." *I'm done,* I thought.

I was groggy but able to answer, though even talking hurt my head more. It felt like they had asked me these questions a few times, and I was growing more and more weary of them.

Doug had driven by himself seventy-eight miles from Orange City hospital to the Sanford hospital in Sioux Falls. He must have been experiencing post-traumatic stress because years earlier, Doug's dad had been airlifted to Sioux Falls, and his dad died on the flight. He later relayed to me that as he drove to meet me, his worry heightened. He prayed the entire way there that I would be alive when he arrived. His memory of not being able to say goodbye to his dad haunted him. When all this was happening with me, Doug was in shock.

The weekend had been normal and pleasant just a few hours earlier. When he told me about his trip, I cried, sad he had to relive the memory of the loss of his father. I know that was difficult for him. Doug told me that they were doing more tests to determine if there was any damage to my brain and to know how to proceed with treatment. The reality of my situation scared me too, which only brought more tears.

Crying, I said to Doug, "I know people who have died instantly from an aneurysm, but mine was a cerebral hemorrhage...Do you know the difference? Do you think I'm going to be okay?"

"The doctors plan to run more tests to see what happened and how it needs to be treated," Doug continued. "You are in the place you need to be right now."

I remained in ICU for almost a week. I was surrounded by flowers that friends had sent. I loved the gifts and sentiments. Even though I was put on stronger pain meds, I still had pain and sensitivity to light and sound. When the monitor by my bed for fluids and heart monitoring would beep, I would lose it and start crying and grumbling out loud. I was getting angry at any sound because it hurt, and I eventually asked for headphones to block sound. Wearing them was the only way I could rest. They gave me a washcloth to put over my eyes, headphones, and turned the lights off in the room because every little thing caused pain. They started me on morphine. I began hallucinating—seeing and hearing things. I had strange things happen during the night because of all the drugs. Some I'm not sure if they were real or not.

They wouldn't let Doug stay in my room, but one night after what may have been a hallucination or a bad dream, I called him at 2 a.m. The last overnight I was there, they let him stay with me because of his inability to rest at home from his worry.

Later, they determined that I was going to be able to recover at home. They also said that the blood would just take time to reabsorb into my brain. Recovering at home with no activity was what was written on my instructions as I was released to recover. They said that the good news was that it wasn't an aneurysm, and so it really shouldn't happen again. They weren't clear why it happened in the first place.

At home, I had all my pain meds that Doug picked up in Sioux Falls. When I got home, I went straight to bed. I had not been able to keep food down when I was in the hospital, and at home it was no different. I didn't mind losing a little weight, but this way was not the way I would have chosen to slim down.

Doug put my flowers in my room so I could look at them. At one point, I looked around my room and thought, *I could have been in a funeral home,* but here I was, alive. I thanked God for my life. I did, however, need to continue the morphine for the pain the first week that I was resting at home.

While I was on the morphine at home, I would hear things like heavy equipment or a song playing, and I would ask Doug about the noise. He said that there was no sound. There were quite a few instances during which I heard things no one else did. I guess I was experiencing more hallucinations. These were frustrating, but the pain was slowly decreasing with rest and pain meds. I was not, however, even close to back to normal.

I had a follow-up appointment on Friday, September 9, 2022— only ten days after I came home from the hospital to recover. During that appointment, I asked if I could travel because my mom had called that day while I was resting. My dad who had been on hospice had taken a turn for the worse. The doctor advised caution in traveling but she wasn't going to tell me no because she could tell I was determined. My mom told me I didn't need to come in my condition, but my gut and Doug's experience with his own dad told me that I needed to go.

The next day, Doug put an air mattress and blankets and pillows in the back of our vehicle so I could lay down and continue to recover on the trip. He drove 300 miles to get me to see my dad. When I got there, Dad was awake but couldn't talk, and they had him on a hospital bed in their living room. My mom was clearly worn out from taking care of my dad during the previous few years, but the last month had been particularly taxing.

I sat with my dad and prayed out loud for him when I got there. Not only was I concerned for him, but my mom told me he was worried about me too. As I prayed for him and held his hand, a tear came to his eye. His tear prompted tears of my own because I knew he was nearing the end. I was glad that he had heard me, and I hugged him gently. I knew what was coming. He had suffered from COPD the previous few years. He had survived the Covid years, but his oxygen levels were decreasing and would not get better.

My mom was feeling the stress of taking care of my dad, and she could no longer do it. Dad also needed a better supply of oxygen. To help Mom rest and give Dad what he needed, hospice care was called to transport him by ambulance to a care facility.

When the ambulance arrived to take Dad to the care facility, the hospice staff, along with the ambulance crew, were there to carry him out on a gurney. They stopped on the front porch to ask if anyone wanted to give him a hug before he left. I took my dad's hand, leaned over him, hugged him gently, and told him again that I loved him. My heart was breaking, and my emotions were raw. I said goodbye as they put him in the ambulance. I began crying uncontrollably as they closed the door because I knew he was even closer to the end. Doug and my brother comforted me.

I was barely able to process what was going on because I was so worn out. I watched the ambulance as it drove away until I couldn't see it anymore. As it disappeared I cried more thinking, *Dad has always been invincible to me, but now he is so frail.* I felt so sad in my heart fearing that I may never see him again.

I was beyond exhausted from my brain bleed, traveling, and the emotions of my dad in hospice—all of it had finally gotten the best of me. I had to go rest for my own recovery. I planned to go see him at the care facility the next day. I got up the next morning, still battle worn, but letting my family know that I wanted to go see Dad.

My mom and my brother shared that he had passed, and that I couldn't see him right then. She said, the ambulance came and transported him from the care facility to the funeral home. I could see him there. I couldn't believe that I wasn't in the facility when he passed away on Monday, September 12, 2022, even though I had travelled all that way to see him. I will never forget that dagger to my heart.

That weekend was so much to take in and a complete blur at the same time. I was very aware of how precious life is for everyone—especially since I had only experienced my own near-death experience less than two weeks earlier. Dad had left Earth to be with the Lord. I was grateful that I hadn't waited to go see him, but I was exceedingly shaky both physically and emotionally. As I mentioned, all this happened within two weeks from when I'd been released from the hospital with my own near-death experience.

The day after Dad passed, Doug took me and my mom to town to begin to make funeral arrangements and make sure everyone knew. Doug called our pastor, who had visited me in the hospital. The church put us all on their prayer list for my continued healing and the grief that my family was feeling. Doug then had to drive back to get our daughter Olivia from college. Cooper took off work, too, and they all rode together to my mom's.

I was so glad to see them when they arrived; their presence strengthened me. The next few days, which involved not only my father's funeral but also interacting with people when I was barely able to function, continued to be a blur.

During the events of those two weeks, I was like a car running on fumes. I made it through, but not without a desperate need to refuel. Though I had pain both physically and emotionally, I was glad to still be on Earth and with my family.

It would take me months to feel better physically, and I still have a hole in my heart from the loss of my dad. I decided to live the rest of my life counting each day with gratitude and I could only think, *Life is fragile and precious.* I had a new appreciation for life. Gratitude and kindness were on the top of my list to practice the rest of my life because you never know what day will be the last. I do know that I want to leave a legacy to my children and friends as my father did to me.

Çhapter N̦ineteen

BECOMING TERESA

A fter I marked the one-year anniversary of my health scare and my father's death, I recovered both physically and emotionally for the most part. I was grateful for my life, and I was feeling good and "normal." "The Webster Dictionary online defines normal as "conforming to type, standard, or regular pattern: characterized by that which is considered usual, typical, or routine."

Most of my life, normal seemed like where I wanted to be and something to strive for. I learned along the way that we are all like snowflakes: different and unique. We were created for our own purpose, and that is enough.

Finding my normal began with acknowledging my illness and my pain. It also involved the need for forgiveness, both for myself and others. I then discovered that for me, true healing required divine intervention, by finding solace and strength in my relationship with God. Through faith, I learned to confront my past, including the struggles with bipolar disorder and the creation of coping mechanisms like the Toni persona.

As I grew spiritually, relying more on faith than fear, I experienced personal growth and authentic self-expression. My path to redemption involved embracing my identity as a beloved child of God and allowing His guidance into every aspect of my life. This spiritual awakening was intensified by a near-death experience that reinforced my desire to live and live purposefully.

I came to understand that life's challenges were part of my journey, shaping me into the person God intended me to be. Throughout this process of becoming Teresa, I learned to trust in God's plan, rely on the Holy Spirit for guidance, and find strength in my faith to overcome obstacles.

I am so glad Doug, the kids, and I weathered the storm and that he and I fit together so well now. We both had our challenges, but isn't that life?

I believe there are some situations that only God can handle.

I continue to work at being my true and authentic self and sometimes that requires going backwards, healing, and then going forward.

I hope you have enjoyed my journey toward "normal," and more importantly, I pray that you are on your path of healing and leveling your mind with God.

I am in a group of women writers called *The Warrior Writers*, who are amazing and encouraging as we pen our books together. Once a week, we do inner healing, which helps replace our thoughts with more positive thoughts with God. The sweet woman who does it for us confirmed that healing isn't a one-and-done, but it is a lifestyle. I was encouraged through people, reading, and looking at myself, so that I could move forward with not only bipolar but with everything else that life presents.

Forty years have passed since I thought there was no hope left and my suicide attempt and diagnosis. Twenty years have passed since I felt there was no hope left in my marriage, and two years have gone by since I thought I might die. All these things had the power to send my life backwards, but through God it has moved my life forward. Those were some of the worst times I had to navigate and could have destroyed me. I can see now that God, Jesus, and the Holy Spirit held a constant place in my heart. God knew what I had to walk through to get to the other side, and He knew what I would need to learn along the way.

Recently, Doug and I celebrated our thirty-second wedding anniversary. We are enjoying each other's company more than ever, and we plan to grow old together. Our kids turned out great! Cooper graduated college with a psychology degree and helps third grade students who need academic help in an elementary school. He is like a gentle giant. Olivia graduated college and is now in the workforce at a Christian book publisher. I am sure that she will serve in other ministry fields as well.

The kids know that they are free to talk about our family's journey with Doug and I as they become young adults in their own relationships. God really is good all the time! He can shape us and mold us in every challenge in our lives. I wouldn't go back and change the journey because it has made us the stronger and more faith-filled people we are today.

C hapter Twenty

PUTTING THE PIECES BACK TOGETHER: A FAMILY'S JOURNEY TOWARD PEACE

D ealing with the marital woes we had affected the entire family—and so does living with a person who has been diagnosed with bipolar. Having grace and a forgiving heart is a must, but it isn't easy.

I asked my family about what these seasons of life were like for them. As I wrap up this book and they pen their words, it is 2025, Doug is sixty-one. Cooper is thirty, Olivia is twenty-three, and I am sixty-four. As we as a family have reflected on crucial times in our lives when we all were younger, we know we are putting words to the wisdom we gained. As I read their words, and as I know you will see as well, God did not just begin to level my mind as we found a new normal, but He began to heal our entire family.

In Doug's words about our marriage troubles, looking back:

My wife asked if I would consider writing a chapter in her book. There is no pressure, and I am under no obligation to do so. In all honesty, I don't really want to; I've been putting it off for months. I've watched as she has relived things throughout the course of writing this book, things I know both of us would just as soon forget and never think about again. The terrible decisions that I made still cause me great remorse, and I assume they always will. I have tended to beat myself up for a mistake over and over again, especially when the mistake was as big as the one I made. Teresa is a one-of-a-kind, strong person, so if she can put herself through what she is by writing this book, to help others, it's time for me to suck it up and see where this goes.

I had an affair. I left my wife and children. I have no excuses, only regrets. This book is about bipolar disorder and, in some parts, the effects it has on those who are with the person who has bipolar disorder.

Let me be clear: I didn't do the things I did because my wife has bipolar. Can she be difficult to live with at times? Sure. But it is no more difficult than I am to live with, and I don't have bipolar. So, while it would be easy to use that as a reason, I can't, I won't. I have no excuses, as I stated.

Somehow, by the grace of God, we are together, even after all that happened. Our kids, too, by the grace of God, survived. They are strong, a beautiful young man and young woman, who are finding their way in life. Neither of them hate me, even though they would have every reason to. I'm lucky and blessed to still be in my wife's life as a husband and in my grown children's lives as their father, I'm not sure I still feel like I deserve it. Teresa is probably the most forgiving person I know, I'm not sure if the shoe had been on the other foot that I would have been able to do the same. I thank God for her and her faith. She is why the kids are okay; she is why we are still married.

How and why the affair happened is not a road I plan to travel. In all honesty, I have blocked a lot of it from my memory. Teresa would tell you that I have more useless sports facts in my brain than the average person. I pull them out all the time, but that's not the case with the affair. Those memories are gone, locked away; they only cause pain, so what's the point? The affair happened; I made really bad, regrettable, selfish decisions because I was weak and lost my way, depending on myself instead of my risen Lord and Savior when times around the house got a little tough. So don't expect a bunch of gory details because there are none to share. This chapter is about hope and healing.

To put an actual finger on what got us back together is difficult. In all honesty, as I remember it, the divorce papers were ready to be signed. I know there was a lot of prayer for reconciliation from multiple people, and especially Teresa never stopped praying. For that, I am grateful. I was working and living in Hull, Iowa, having left the company I had been at for all of the twenty years of my career prior (another bad decision on my part), and Teresa, Cooper, and Olivia still lived in our home in Orange City, Iowa. I was lonely, and my life was empty. At several times during the time we were apart, I actually told God I really didn't want to be here on Earth anymore. Fortunately, His plans are better than mine, and I didn't act upon my thoughts.

Teresa and I had started to spend more and more time together that summer when we were separated, especially with the kids. Walls had been put up; trust had been broken and lost. It was awkward at times; I was dealing with a tremendous amount of guilt——the reasons for that guilt would make a list that goes on and on.

Teresa and I were never great at communicating to begin with, and then throw in ten tons of baggage, and connecting becomes a monumental feat to try and overcome. Somehow, we came to the decision that we both still wanted to try and make things work, and that I would move back home.

It was weird, hard, and definitely uncomfortable at times. Our family and friends didn't know how to handle it. It's not just like you snap your fingers, click your heels and things are back to normal. I still feel bad to this day about what I put all of them through as well.

Some of the relationships with other couples have never been the same, and I deeply regret that. We live in a small town, and even things like going back to church were hard for me. I felt judged, and rightfully so; people had every right to question where my head and heart were. I understood that the reason for their apprehension was on me, but it added to my insecurities and the uphill climb that I had to make to get back to the place where I could even be a fraction of the husband and father that Teresa, Cooper, and Olivia deserved.

Much tension was present as I transitioned back into the family. I was also dealing with so much anger at many things, but mostly at myself. Unfortunately, the anger came out more often than I would like, and it was unfairly directed at Teresa and others.

In addition to the uncertainty of whether or not this new situation would be a permanent one, our kids had to endure a different kind of pain once I was in the house. Olivia recently shared that while she obviously saw us fight, a lot, she never saw us make up. She knew we got past the fight, or at least assumed we did, but she never experienced us making up firsthand. That was a punch in the stomach for me, but what a courageous thing for her to tell us. *How unfair,* I thought. Their dad had left once already, I wonder how many nights she and Cooper went to bed wondering if their dad was going to leave again after a disagreement between their mother and father.

I now am keenly aware that kids need to see their parents make up, hug, kiss, hold hands, and have a kind word; they deserve to know it's going to be alright. Our kids especially deserved that reassurance, and the lack of that was another big miss on my part. There's the old saying, "Don't go to bed angry" at your spouse, but you also need to make sure your kids know things are okay. They have enough to deal with in this crazy world without having to worry about their parents on top of everything else. To add to everything, things weren't going great with my job either. I was extremely unhappy on that front. It just added to my tension and anger.

Then a true God thing happened. I was talking, or should I say complaining, to Teresa one night after work. She patiently listened, but then she finally looked at me and said it's time for you to go back to your old company. The very next day, I already had a lunch scheduled with a dear friend from there. I was going on, and on about how challenging things were and how unhappy I was, and with no knowledge of the conversation that was held the previous evening, he looked at me and said, "It's time for you to come back to work with us."

This move wasn't without its challenges, but the ball started rolling, and God opened doors, and I did land back there. That was eleven years ago, and I'm still there. I thank God for making that happen, as it was a key part of my restoration journey.

There was still a big hurdle to overcome, though. I was still just angry, all the time. The anger was always right there at the surface, and any little thing would trigger it—I mean anything—could set me off. I needed help, even though stubbornly I thought I could get through it on my own; after all, I'm supposed to be a tough, smart man. As much as I wanted that, it wasn't going to happen on my own.

Finally, Teresa convinced me to start seeing someone that we both knew and that she had worked with, a faith-based coach and mentor. We started drilling into the root of my anger. It came down to forgiveness. Teresa told me all the time that she had forgiven me, but I was unable or unwilling to accept it. Even though the things I did weren't very Christ-like, I am a Christian, and I know the good book tells me that if I confess my sins, God forgives me. As one of my good friends likes to say—grace, upon grace, upon grace, upon grace. So even with all this going for me, there is no way I could find the ability to forgive myself. None of this should have happened; this was my fault; I hurt people. If I keep this at the forefront and keep beating myself up over it time and time again, I ensure it never happens again.

My counselor stayed after me and kept challenging me. I kept praying and reading and eventually was able to come to the realization that my attitude, my need to punish myself, was only hurting me and everyone else around me. I couldn't move forward, and neither could this marriage with this constant weight around my neck. I had to give it over to God, to lay it at the foot of the cross. Don't get me wrong, to this day, I still ask myself from time to time. *Why did I make the choices I made? How dumb am I? How selfish?* During those times, I have to go back to the fact that God has forgiven me; I needed to forgive myself. I turned it over to Him and forgave myself.

I'm a hard person to live with, always have been. I know it—I have always known it. My anger still surfaces too often. I can be quiet and moody. I'm not a big talker to begin with, and I go inside my head and worry way too much about things I don't need to worry about, especially if I truly trusted and handed things over to my heavenly Father.

Bless her heart, Teresa puts up with me. Like I said, my purpose in writing my section of this chapter is hope and healing, I'm still amazed and blessed that she took me back. Is our marriage perfect? Far from it, and I just described a bunch of the reasons why. We're still a work in progress. I suppose we always will be, and that's okay.

We are content but not complacent. I wish I had known the things I know now back when we were married in our thirties. I wish my faith—our faith—was then what it is now.

What if, what if…it doesn't do any good to dwell on the past? I've learned that we can't go back; only forward. We must continue to learn, to forgive, to surround ourselves with strong people of faith.

185

Most importantly, for Teresa and I, we need to communicate, lean on each other, be there for each other, pray together and for each other, and love each other, for better or worse, just like we committed to in our wedding vows.

By the grace of God, we are going to make it, and our children are going to be okay, and I'm blessed as a result. I love you, Teresa! Thanks for being my wife—Doug

In Olivia's words about our marriage troubles, looking back:

Would I have been more scarred knowing the truth right away or finding out later that a piece of my carefully crafted reality was a lie?

My father cheated on my mom when I was a child. This affair took place for a whole year before he decided to tell my mom the truth. The other woman was someone from his work, and to this very day, the other woman lives in the next town over.

All of these details were revealed to me a few weeks ago.

I love my parents, and I thank God every day that He put me in this family. Both of my parents love me immensely, and I wish I could do a better job at showing them my love and appreciation back.

When I was younger, I was such a handful because I constantly craved love; however, I conveyed this in a very sassy way that involved the constant use of "whatever" and slamming doors. As twenty-two-year-old me looks back at that little girl, I feel an inkling of sadness. I demanded words of affirmation when my parents were struggling the most with loving each other.

It wasn't until I came to college and started going to Chi Alpha, my campus ministry organization, that I was introduced to vulnerability. For a long time, I thought I was vulnerable because I would tell anyone anything. However, vulnerability wasn't my best friend—transparency was. Even to this day, I have a nasty habit of telling people what I went through instead of what I'm going through. God revealed to me that I'm really prideful when it comes to self-knowledge. As a result, I have the tendency to cry alone and then reach out to my community only after I've determined what pushed me over the edge, the core reason, and how to proceed.

I don't remember many events from the time my father was gone, but I remember one time when he brought me to the condo he was staying in at the time. I always fell asleep during the car ride, so I thought he was taking my brother and me on his business trip with him. I don't know how far away we were, but I felt very lonely without my mom. I remember crying relentlessly and wishing she would just appear.

During these early years of my life, I would keep a picture of my mom in my nightstand drawer even though she was just down the hall. Although I love my father and brother, my mom has always been a constant in my life. She worked at the elementary school when I was attending, and even when she was no longer at her job, she would drop me off at school every morning. This was a pattern until my last two years of high school when I finally decided I was brave enough to drive to school myself. So that night without even a glimpse of mom was highly unusual.

As a small child, I didn't realize what was happening. I thought the whole world revolved around me. It was because of these overwhelming feelings, combined with the secrets surrounding our family, that I thought that every tear shed was caused by me. It felt as if every time I spoke, someone in the family ended up crying...even if that person was me.

In Cooper's words about our marriage troubles, looking back:

I don't always remember everything that happened back then. My memory can be kind of foggy, especially when it comes to stuff that was stressful or upsetting. But I do remember certain things, and they've stayed with me.

I remember how my mom used to get really moody and upset, especially during the time when my dad wasn't living at home. I was just a kid—hadn't even gone through puberty yet—but I ended up taking on this role, trying to be "the man of the house." I wasn't a man, but Mom said I was big and strong, and she asked me to help. I did what I could. I tried to comfort her when she was upset, talk her down, help her feel better. But I realize now that it wasn't really my job to do that.

I have good memories, too, despite their separation. Mom and I watched a lot of movies together. I liked that—just spending time with her—but I didn't like feeling like I had to carry the weight of helping her feel okay. That wasn't supposed to be my responsibility.

There's one memory that I've reminded Mom about so many times over the years. I'll say, "Mom, do you remember when you were so mad at Dad, and you threw my fish bowl with my beta fish and the plant off the counter?" The fish didn't make it. And until we got new flooring, there was this chip in the tile that always reminded me of that day. It felt like everything in our family broke a little bit then.

I'm kind of like Mom in that I tend to block out the really bad or upsetting things. But I do remember hearing her and Dad's arguments. I would listen in, trying to figure out what was going on, feeling anxious and scared. Even now, if there's an argument or a tense situation, I get really uncomfortable. It brings me back to that feeling of not knowing what was going to happen next.

I know Mom tried to make things better. She signed me up for Big Brothers and Big Sisters so I could have someone to talk to and hang out with. I really liked that. It helped a lot.

Olivia and I know that we can talk about these past traumas with Mom and Dad at any time. Our healing is very important to them.

Aren't my kids amazing and mature? How they turned out despite everything is the biggest demonstration of God's grace in my life.

You may also be wondering, "How did your children weather your storm of bipolar and 'find normal' too?"

I knew about my experience growing up with my mom, who we later learned had bipolar, but I wanted to know my kids' experiences too. Even though by their writing and by what I see they both appear to be doing well as young adults, a parent always wonders, *Did I do a good job, in spite of myself and my struggles along the way?*

To find out, after I read their words about the aftermath of our separation, I asked them three additional questions to help me and readers further understand what their experience was like living with a parent with bipolar.

Here are the questions and Olivia's answers:

- **What have you learned or felt while growing up with a mom who has bipolar disorder?**

  Growing up, I had really strong emotions, but I didn't know how to handle them. Our household showed a lot of emotions to one another, but, honestly, we didn't talk about them. Although K-12 was really hard, God has redeemed a part of me...I used to loathe my sensitivity, and I often wished that I didn't care as much as I did. However, God has made that part of me—the emotional part—my biggest strength when connecting to other people. Honestly, if I didn't grow up with an emotionally intense family, I probably wouldn't be the person I am today. I still look back and feel a little sad and pitiful toward the little girl I once was. Remembering her cry and in pain because she felt like no one could understand her is still hard, but I don't think I could change anything because of how blessed and transformed I am today through Jesus Christ.

190

- **Can you remember a time when you saw God at work in our family, even during a hard moment?**

Last year, I decided to go all-in on my relationship with the Lord. Before that, I was half-committed and still torn between my worldly desires and God's desire to call me higher. The first time I came home last year was a really tough one. I've often heard people say that the closer we get to God, the more we realize how we aren't like Him. Not only was that true for me, but it became true for my family as well. No family is perfect. We should never expect our families to be perfect because we are all broken people. However, we should also not get comfortable with our dysfunction, and trust me, every family is a little dysfunctional.

I distinctly remember going home and telling my family all about my church's winter conference. I was raving about the Lord and His goodness. I remember my father turned to my mom and said something along the lines of, "Mother, your daughter is all about the Lord now." The way he said it wasn't exactly positive or negative.

My parents have always believed in the Lord, and I'm grateful to have been raised in a Christian household. However, we were getting used to sitting in our dysfunction. It was easy to stay home from church, reading the Bible every day wasn't talked about, and bad habits just seemed too difficult to break. I remember leaving home after winter break, worried. I was worried that I wouldn't enjoy going home anymore. The closer I got to the Lord, the more I wanted to bring every conversation back to Him. At the time, I didn't see the same thought process when talking to my parents.

I don't know what happened in between then and the next time I came home, but I know that only the Lord could have done it. I don't go home regularly, so the next time I went home would have been, probably four or five months later. Although they were still my family, something had changed. As my mom began working on her book and meeting with faith-driven women, her faith also started coming to the surface. My father's community began to grow, and he became friends with people who challenged him in his faith. Having my parents grow in their faith at the same time I was growing in mine, was, and still is, the biggest blessing I could ever ask for.

- **If someone else was growing up with a parent with bipolar, what would you tell them to give them hope?**

For the child who is scared of being forgotten and big emotions, I would just like to say that it'll get easier for both you and your parent. A good friend of mine once told me, "Remember that both you and your parents are living life for the first time." This truth rings in my mind frequently because it's a reminder that we need to give grace to ourselves and to others.

As the years passed, I learned how to process big emotions and how to communicate with my parents. At the same time, my mom was learning and growing in her own way. She was figuring out how to be a mom of two kids while also struggling with bipolar depression. She was learning how to search for God even when the world seemed dark.

We're all living life for the first time. There are going to be mistakes and trauma, because everyone has some kind of family trauma, but the best part is that the Lord is going to use it all for our good and His glory. He is the most amazing and best kind of author because He can take the parts of our lives that we wanted to erase and turn them into a testimony that we can't stop sharing.

Here are the questions and Cooper's answers:

- **What have you learned or felt while growing up with a mom who has bipolar disorder?**

I remember when my mom would get upset and I was in my room. I would turn down the volume on a game I was playing and try to listen. Then I would try to be a mediator. I was hyper-vigilant when my parents would argue because of my mom's bipolar. She would repeat herself and get so worked up in a frenzy that things escalated. Though I wanted to step in and help with the situation, I learned that it wasn't a good idea, and many times, it only made it worse. So, my suggestion is don't try to be a mediator.

- **Can you remember a time when you saw God at work in our family, even during a hard moment?**

God helped my mom when she went through many troubled times in her life and even when she had a brain bleed recently. He guarded and protected her but also taught her lessons along the way. God also brought my dad back so that we could be a family again and my mom could have the support that she needed.

- **If someone else was growing up with a parent with bipolar, what would you tell them to give them hope?**

Bipolar didn't define my mom, and I could tell that she always wanted to be better. It never changed her love for us, her desire to be a family, and her choice to be the best mom she could be. I would say though that it is good to let your parents know that as children you absorb more and hear more than they think you do. If they are going to fight around their children, they should also make up around their children, so the kids know everything is okay. You can always be a family and support each other in good times and bad. Cherish the good memories.

Chapter Twenty-one

AN INVITATION TO MOVE CLOSER TO THE "NORMAL" GOD INTENDED FOR YOU

Thank you for coming along on my journey. I hope you also enjoyed my family's account of how their lives were affected. Bipolar not only affects the person diagnosed but those close to them. If you have walked with me to this point, I believe it is likely because you—or someone you love—has struggled with bipolar.

As you can see from my story, finding normal can be a lengthy up-and-down process. I pray that this story finds you prior to a suicide attempt or a crumbling of a marriage. But if not, I hope you will see God's amazing love, His ongoing faithfulness, His healing power, and the truth that *victory is possible* in spite of any diagnosis.

I am a living testimony that God was always there to level my mind, guiding me to various models of therapy at just the right times. He also had amazing professionals and friends come alongside me along the way. And despite everything I dealt with, He did give me the normal I sought—and so much more.

It took every ounce of what God taught me through my grandma and others—to persevere no matter what life brought my way. As I've shared, I've now lived more than forty years with a bipolar diagnosis, and the lessons are clear to me in hindsight!

I pray that my story enables you to find normal and beyond much more quickly!

In fact, I am confident that God will use this book and my life to spare others a portion of the struggles that I had to endure. He helps us comfort others with the comfort that we find from Him.

To begin finding normal, I encourage you to ask for something even better—something I wish I had found earlier—a deeper relationship with God.

To that end, I'd like to offer a prayer for you:

Father, I lift up the readers of this book to you. May Your love surround them and may Your peace level their minds. Order their steps as they take their first steps toward healing. Guide their futures and give them courage to keep going. Give them the strength they need to overcome mental illness and assure them with Your love and with the help of others around them that they are never alone.

Bless their purposes, Lord, and help them live out what normal looks like in the ways You have created them.
Be with the loved ones of those fighting the battle so that they can link arms with those struggling and help them navigate their futures together.

Fill everyone who is reading this prayer with hope, healing, and the joy of walking closely with You that You have for them.

In Jesus' name, I pray, Amen.

I know the Lord will begin to answer this prayer for you, just as He did for me. If I could sit with you across the table and have a cup of coffee, in the waiting, however, I would say, sometimes faith feels intangible when life is overwhelming.

We, however, can help make faith more practical as we implement simple strategies confirmed by God's Word into our daily routines. I initially thought routines and discipline were limiting; perhaps you may feel that way too. I now, however, have experienced how important they are in freeing us and helping us become steadier.

I have used ten key areas to bring about that discipline for myself. These strategies are rooted in wisdom, tested in my life, and strengthened by God's Word.

I encourage you to ask the Lord to highlight one area to focus on at a time; don't feel pressure to do them all at once. Just do your best each day, and after the first strategy you chose becomes a habit, add another, and then another. Over time, you may find that you have greater balance, joy, and peace than you ever imagined on your way to a relationship with God and being authentically you. I hope these life-giving routines bless you as they have me on my journey. The most important thing is to progress at your own pace and make the routine a habit before moving on to the next. Don't give up, don't give in, and continue to move forward in a positive way. I believe in you.

TEN STRATEGIES TO LEVEL THE MIND WITH GOD'S LOVE AND PEACE

1. **Get Rest.**

   Sleep is essential for both physical and emotional stability. When we trust God enough to slow down and sleep, it reminds us that He is in control, even when our minds race.

   Getting good rest was a struggle for me and I know it can be for others but remember, rest helps stabilize moods. I have a bedtime reminder on my phone to start winding down for bed, and prayers and that helps me. If I don't get enough rest, unsteady moods are more likely to occur.

   "Come to me, all you who are weary and burdened,
   and I will give you rest."
   (Matthew 11:28)

2. **Eat Right.**

   Nutrition affects mood and energy. Choosing healthy foods can be an act of self-care, inviting God into the daily choices that support stability and well-being.

   I love all kinds of food, but I have noticed that I feel better when I eat fruits and vegetables. I also drink enough water to stay hydrated. The body is a temple to be honored and taken care of, as I often remind myself.

   "So whether you eat or drink or whatever you do, do it
   all for the glory of God."
   (1 Corinthians 10:31)

3. **Exercise.**

    Exercise helps regulate emotions, reduce anxiety, and relieve tension. Moving your body can be like a prayer in motion, a way to say thank you, Lord for this body and the strength you give.

    I used to exercise more robustly when I was younger but now I still enjoy golfing, walking, and housework as my daily exercise. As I take the time to walk and golf, I marvel at the majesty of God's creation in my surroundings.

    > *"Do you not know that your bodies are temples of the Holy Spirit, who is in you, whom you have received from God? You are not your own."*
    > (1 Corinthians 6:19)

4. **Breathe Deeply.**

    During stress or mania, slowing your breath helps ground you. Practicing deep, mindful breathing is a way to quiet racing thoughts. Remember God's calming presence with every inhale and exhale.

    Taking a few minutes to slow down and intentionally breathe deeply when I'm stressed can make a big difference. It is a welcome reprieve from daily busyness. I remind myself that I can do it anywhere.

    > *"Be still, and know that I am God; I will be exalted among the nations, I will be exalted in the earth."*
    > (Psalm 46:10)

5. **Pray/Spend Time with God.**

Bipolar can make spiritual rhythms challenging, but even short prayers or scriptures help center you. Making time for God daily anchors you in His unchanging love. Even when moods feel unpredictable.

I love short devotionals, daily calendars with scripture, and listening to the Bible on Audible. I can always stop for a short infusion of God throughout the day and listening versus reading keeps my attention better.

"Your word is a lamp for my feet, a light on my path."
(Psalm 119:105)

6. **Listen to Worship Music.**

Soothing sounds and words can counter anxiety or agitation. Worship music especially turns focus from fear to faith, inviting God's peace to fill troubled thoughts.

When I am in a "funk" and my moods are down or unpredictable, I turn up the worship music and shut out the noise of the world. Listening to this kind of music replaces that noise with truth and hope.

"Come, let us sing for joy to the LORD; let us shout aloud to the Rock of our salvation."
(Psalm 95:1)

7. **Do Progressive Relaxation.**

Stress tightens the body and mind. Gently relaxing each muscle slowly, while inviting Holy Spirit's comfort, helps to release tension and to restore peace.

I used guided audio to help my body gradually and intentionally relax and unwind. It is important to take time to unwind and relax. This relaxation is even helpful at bedtime to fall asleep.

> *"Therefore do not worry about tomorrow, for tomorrow will worry about itself. Each day has enough trouble of its own."*
> (Matthew 6:34)

8. **Use Inner Healing or Therapy.**

Bipolar can uncover deep wounds or regrets, bringing these to God for healing through prayer, counseling, or community opens the door to His transformative grace.

I love my time with the Warrior Writer support community, where I get inner healing, prayer, and support for not just my writing journey but for life. Continued therapy and working on healing have made all the difference for me. Finding a support system in the form of a like-minded community was a key component for me and perhaps it will be for you too.

> *"Heal me, LORD, and I will be healed; save me and I will be saved, for you are the one I praise."*
> (Jeremiah 17:14)

9. **Practice Positive Self-Talk.**

When self-critical or racing thoughts overwhelm, speaking God's truth over yourself is vital. Say out loud: "I am loved, I am chosen, and I am not my diagnosis; His grace is sufficient for me!"

I like to call this mirror time when I speak encouragements directly to myself in the mirror at home or in the car. I tell myself, "God loves you, and you are enough just being you." It helps me know he always has my back and to just relax and be the authentic me He created.

"This is the day the LORD has made; let us rejoice and be glad in it."
(Psalm 118:24 ESV)

10. Show Gratitude.

Even in episodes of depression or mania, gratitude shifts our perspective. Listing blessings daily—no matter how small— helps refocus on God's faithfulness and bring light into dark moments.

When I choose gratitude, I find joy creeping in. Gratitude changes the atmosphere and steers me away from negativity and toward light. Many times I even have to take a break from negative people for my own well-being.

"Give thanks to the LORD, for he is good; his love endures forever."
(Psalm 107:1)

As I finish writing this book, my heart is full of gratitude—for God's patience with me, for His Word that steadies me, and for His Spirit that whispers peace to me in times of trouble. I also carry gratitude for you, my reader, for being willing to walk through these pages. I hope and pray that it helped you in your journey.

May these ten practices help you not only manage life with bipolar disorder, but may they help you discover the joy of living more fully in Christ.

If I could offer one more parting piece of encouragement: Be persistent in your journey with the Peace-giver at the center of your life. To help with that process, I offer three of my favorite passages from His Word:

> *"Consider it pure joy, my brothers and sisters, whenever you face trials of many kinds, because you know that the testing of your faith produces perseverance. Let perseverance finish its work so that you may be mature and complete, not lacking anything."*
> (James:1:2–4)

> *"Have I not commanded you? Be strong and courageous. Do not be afraid; do not be discouraged, for the LORD your God will be with you wherever you go."*
> (Joshua 1:9)

> *"For I know the plans I have for you," declares the LORD, "plans to prosper you and not to harm you, plans to give you hope and a future."*
> (Jeremiah 29:11)

I also know, that if you are like me, you may likely be your own worst critic when you don't follow through in your attempts to improve. I get it. I've been there over and over again. But God is always faithful to help us try again when we turn back to Him. That's why I'm sharing a prayer of surrender that I use when I depart from God's ways to help me reconnect with Him. If you feel like you have strayed from Him or if you are struggling to follow God's leading, I invite you to pray:

Father, I am sorry that I have not always rested in You and that I have tried to figure out things on my own without asking You. I confess that I let sadness, a diagnosis, stress, and the troubles of life to get me down. From this day forward, I will make a conscious decision to remember that I am Yours and You are mine. I know that You will protect me from harm. Thank You for Jesus who shows me how to love and surrender to You.

In His name, I pray. Amen.

AN OFFER FOR ADDITIONAL HELP

Part of moving forward in life, as you know by now, is to seek help from others who have walked in the journey you find yourself on. Making progress also involves knowing the stage we are currently in. Though I couldn't help anyone navigating mental illness too early in my journey, I am equipped as I finish this book with the Armor of God and everything I have learned during the last forty years.

I have moved from self-doubt and struggle to a life of purpose, resilience, and a deep-seated desire to share my experiences to help others facing the challenges God has enabled me to overcome.

If this book resonated with you, and you want someone to walk you through the ten strategies or other ideas you got from this book, I would love to help you interactively. I am a certified life coach, and I also understand when a person needs professional licensed counseling or help from a doctor.

I'm honored to walk alongside others who are seeking normal with bipolar. As I've mentioned, I'm especially passionate about helping others level their minds and achieve their goals sooner than I did. I know God has amazing plans for you, and that He gives us whoever we may need to assist in the journey.

If you'd like to see if I might be the person that God has in mind to help you or a loved one at this time, I invite you to schedule a free consultation by using the following QR code. There's no obligation to continue. Wherever God leads you for help, may you sense His love and peace on your journey.

Blessings!

Teresa Brunsting

ACKNOWLEDGEMENTS

To my editor and friend, Loral Pepoon: thank you for your keen eye, thoughtful feedback, and steady encouragement. You made this book stronger and clearer.

To Missy Maxwell Worton, Donna Bess, Tammy Largin, and Niccie Kliegl: thank you for believing in this project from the very beginning and all your encouragement and expertise along the way.

A heartfelt thank you to all my friends and writing community, *The Warrior Writers*, for your support, laughter, and honest advice. I'm so grateful for the brainstorming sessions, the shared cups of coffee, and the moments when you reminded me to breathe.

Lastly, to you, the reader: thank you for opening this book and joining me on this journey. Your time, your attention, and your hearts mean everything. I hope these pages offer you encouragement, insight, and perhaps even the comfort of knowing you're not alone.

ABOUT THE AUTHOR

Author and certified life coach Teresa Brunsting is thrilled to debut her first full-length book with *Finding Normal in Bipolar*. Although she loved her twenty-year career working in progressively more advanced roles in computer graphics and training, her favorite roles have been as a wife and mother. That's why she is on a mission to help wives and mothers who are hoping to live out those God-given roles well.

After her own journey in dealing with these already challenging roles with bipolar disorder, she especially has a soft spot for ladies who are still discovering how to cope with fluctuating emotions.

She is grateful for God's grace that has sustained her forty-year journey of living with bipolar. Friends would call her kind, steady, and reliable. She is passionate about sharing her coping strategies and life lessons with others through one-on-one coaching. She imparts lessons to help her clients to come to peace with whatever comes their way, believing God brings good out of every experience.

Writing a book and going back into the most difficult parts of her story has been much more difficult than she thought, but Teresa believes that if she helps one person in the darkest places or on any part of the journey, it will be worth it. She credits her perseverance to relying on God and counting her blessings, principles her beloved grandmother passed down to her.

Teresa's writings have appeared in a magazine entitled *As for Me and My House* and in an anthology called *Resilience* featuring the Warrior Writer community she is blessed to be a part of, led by Missy Maxwell Worton. She has been featured on Parent Compass TV, and she speaks on various women's issues including overcoming bipolar, international adoption, parenting, becoming bold, and the effects of inner healing on mental health.

Teresa is a loving wife to Doug, who she has been married to for three decades, mother to her adult children Cooper and Olivia, and a dog mom to Gracie. Most recently she has become a grand dog mother to her son's dog, Riku.

DEFINITIONS

Definition of Bipolar I and II from Mayo Clinic https://www.mayoclinic.org/diseases-conditions/bipolar-disorder/symptoms-causes/syc-20355955

Bipolar I disorder. You've had at least one manic episode that may come before or after hypomanic or major depressive episodes. In some cases, mania may cause a break from reality. This is called psychosis.

Bipolar II disorder. You've had at least one major depressive episode and at least one hypomanic episode. But you've never had a manic episode.

BP hope magazine website: https://www.bphope.com/

988 Crisis Hotline - https://988lifeline.org/

"At the 988 Suicide & Crisis Lifeline, we understand that life's challenges can sometimes be difficult. Whether you're facing mental health struggles, emotional distress, alcohol or drug use concerns, or just need someone to talk to, our caring counselors are here for you. You are not alone."

A SPECIAL SONG

Because I often felt unloved and with a lack of purpose during parts of my life, I fondly remember one of Grandma's favorite songs, *Amazing Grace*. I too felt lost but now I am found. This song from her old country church reminds me of my journey to find "normal" and leveling my mind. It still rings true in my heart, and I hope as you read the words, it will give you hope too.

Amazing Grace

John Newton, **pub.1779**
v. 7 by Anonymous/Unknown, **pub.1829**

1.
Amazing grace! How sweet the sound
That saved a wretch like me!
I once was lost, but now am found;
Was blind, but now I see.

2.
'Twas grace that taught my heart to fear,
And grace my fears relieved;
How precious did that grace appear
The hour I first believed.

3.
Through many dangers, toils, and snares,
I have already come;
'Tis grace hath brought me safe thus far,
And grace will lead me home.

4.
The Lord has promised good to me,
His Word my hope secures;
He will my Shield and Portion be,
As long as life endures.

5.
Yea, when this flesh and heart shall fail,
And mortal life shall cease,
I shall possess, within the veil,
A life of joy and peace.

6.
The earth shall soon dissolve like snow,
The sun forbear to shine;
But God, who called me here below,
Will be forever mine.

7.
When we've been there ten thousand years,
Bright shining as the sun,
We've no less days to sing God's praise
Than when we'd first begun.

NOTES

According to the Chicago Manual of Style (17th ed.)

1 Mayo Clinic Staff, "Bipolar Disorder," Mayo Clinic, last modified April 7, 2024, https://www.mayoclinic.org/diseases-conditions/bipolar-disorder/symptoms-causes/syc-20355955

2 Ibid.

3 Kendra Cherry, "What Is Attachment Theory?" Verywell Mind, last modified February 14, 2023, https://www.verywellmind.com/what-is-attachment-theory-2795337.

4 World Vision Australia, "40 Years On, the 40 Hour Famine Has Helped Millions," *World Vision*, accessed May 28, 2025, https://www.worldvision.com.au/global-issues/work-we-do/poverty/40-years-on-the-40-hour-famine-helped-millions

5 *Groundhog Day*, directed by Harold Ramis (Culver City, CA: Columbia Pictures, 1993), film.

6 Margaret Mitchell, *Gone with the Wind* (New York: Macmillan, 1936).

7 Heidi Murkoff, Sharon Mazel, and Charles J. Lockwood, *What to Expect* series (various editions; New York: Workman Publishing, various dates).

8 Mayo Clinic Staff, "Autism Spectrum Disorder," *Mayo Clinic*, last modified November 10, 2023, https://www.mayoclinic.org/diseases-conditions/autism-spectrum-disorder/symptoms-causes/syc-20352928.

[9] U.S. Department of Justice, "Section 504, Rehabilitation Act of 1973," *ADA.gov*, accessed May 28, 2025, https://www.ada.gov/.

[10] *It's a Wonderful Life*, directed by Frank Capra (Los Angeles: Liberty Films, 1946), film.

[11] *DreamBible.com*, accessed May 28, 2025, https://www.dreambible.com.

[12] *DreamDictionary.org*, accessed May 28, 2025, https://www.dreamdictionary.org.

[13] Barbie L. Breathitt, *A to Z Dream Symbology Dictionary* (Fort Worth, TX: Breath of the Spirit Ministries, 2011).

[14] "Biblical Meaning of 444," *BiblicalTribe.com*, accessed May 28, 2025, https://biblicaltribe.com/biblical-meaning-of-444/.

[15] *The Shack*, directed by Stuart Hazeldine (Los Angeles: Summit Entertainment, 2017), based on the novel by William P. Young.

[16] Don Miguel Ruiz, *The Four Agreements: A Practical Guide to Personal Freedom* (San Rafael, CA: Amber-Allen Publishing, 1997).

[17] *The Four Cardinal Virtues*, Wikipedia, https://en.wikipedia.org/wiki/Cardinal_virtues.